The Gift of Divorce: A Journey of Empowerment Through Self-Love

Dumari St. Angelo

Beautiful Kelly,
you are awesome,
my friend!
Love,
Dumari ♡

www.EmpowerUFromWithin.com

To my ex-husband, Matt, my soul friend through eternity.
Thank you for all the gifts our journey together offered me.

And to my beloved Spiritual Support Team.
I am deeply grateful for the unconditional love, wise guidance,
and infinite light you bring into my life.
Thank you for always believing in me, even when I didn't.

Table of Contents

Introduction

"With everything that has happened to you,
you can either feel sorry for yourself
or treat what has happened as a gift.
Everything is either an opportunity to grow
or an obstacle to keep you from growing.
You get to choose."

—Wayne Dyer

Two days after Christmas, it was cold outside and there was a light cover of snow on the ground. I lay in my bed underneath the warm comforter, yet feeling cold inside. I was still in my pajamas, and it was well past 10 a.m. I was rarely in bed that late, even on the weekends. I usually get up before 6 a.m., but not on that December day: I had barely slept. The night before had been painful.

Christmas is usually my favorite time of the year, but this had been the saddest holiday season I'd ever experienced. I felt abandoned by the man I used to consider my best friend and life partner. The last few months had been so painful. I was sad and afraid.

I meditated and prayed all morning. I talked to my Spiritual Support Team—my angels and guides—and asked for help, for guidance, for healing. My heart ached, and I knew that I needed help.

Suddenly, I felt a soothing, peaceful energy. I recognized the presence of my Team. I felt my breathing shift. As I began to breathe more deeply, I knew they were helping me to feel the love…the love within me.

They said, *First, accept what is going on. Acceptance is an act of self-love. Accept yourself, forgive yourself, and love yourself. You cannot depend on others for love and acceptance. You are the source of the Love you seek. No one else is. Love is who you are. Still your mind and open your heart to the infinite Love within it.*

They guided me to breathe into my heart. As I breathed, I saw in my mind's eye a flower bud within my heart. It was opening up its petals into a beautiful flower. My heart was opening, and I could sense a warm glow emanating from it. Peace enfolded me. I knew they were reminding me of my innocence and purity. They reminded me that I am divine and that my essence is pure Love. As I breathed, they invited me to relax into this knowing. A sense of wellbeing filled me. I felt Love. I felt loving. I felt loved.

I then heard them say, *Matt's soul is giving you a gift. Love is the answer, and the answer is within you. Your brave journey will connect and strengthen those who are in their darkest moments, when they feel alone and abandoned.*

This was the first time I realized that the challenges I was experiencing within my marriage were a gift. I was starting to get glimpses of this gift. First, I would get to know what loving myself was really like. Then, I would be better able to help others experience loving themselves in a very practical way, and to remind them that they are the source of the love and everything else they seek.

***

My journey through the challenging months before and after that Christmas would have been very different—and more difficult—if I didn't have the inner guidance, higher insights, and divine support I received through that period of time. One of the reasons I was able to move through the experience of my marriage falling apart and eventual divorce in such a positive and empowering way was my strong connection to my Spiritual Support Team. My Team is my inner guidance system!

There were many ways my Team got their messages through to me during this time. Sometimes I got them through my intuitive senses: through visions, thoughts, words within my head (including songs), inner feelings, and my inner knowing. Other times the messages came through my environment: e-mails, books, license plates, people, animals, and more appeared when I needed them most. And sometimes, my Team inspired me with thoughts that seemed like mine, but were coming from a higher place that uplifted me, helped me feel better, and empowered me.

***

I first got introduced to my Spiritual Support Team just before I got married in 1999. I moved to Boston from Puerto Rico when I was twenty to finish my degree in Computer Information Systems. I met Matt in college, and afterwards, we continued our relationship in New Hampshire as we began our careers.

Ever since I was in high school, I've been interested in the spiritual world and have been fascinated by people who could receive messages from angels, spirit guides, and even God.

During my search for spiritual understanding, I found the book *The Lightworker's Way* by Doreen Virtue, Ph.D. Doreen writes about our shared potential for connecting with angels and awakening to our spiritual gifts. I was so excited to discover her work—and even more excited to find out she was offering a course to become a Certified Spiritual Counselor the following month! I wanted to connect with my angels, and I felt a strong need to sign up.

I loved connecting with my angels during class. It felt so right. Over the course of three weekends, I began to get in touch with my Spiritual Team for the first time.

Unfortunately, when I got back home, I found that I was filled with self-doubt when connecting with them. "Did I make that up? Was that real? Can I do it again?" I wondered.

Soon after completing Doreen's class, I got married and had my first boy. I got so involved in my busy, new family life that I "forgot" my angels.

Fast-forward four years: I was really struggling as the new mom of two boys who were challenging me in ways I had never experienced before. I knew I needed extra help. I felt alone, unsupported, and confused. I needed tools to help me tackle the challenges I was facing as a new mom.

I prayed for help, and I was guided not only to parenting tools that helped me, but also and most importantly to reconnect with my angels. As I reconnected with them, I was able to care for my boys and for myself with more grace and ease. I knew I'd never forget about my angels again.

Now, I was ready to go through Doreen's one-week Angel Therapy Practitioner (ATP) training in California. It was the best thing I ever did. That's when I really started experiencing the magic of connecting with and receiving clear messages from my Team. It changed my life.

I later served as volunteer staff in five of Doreen's ATP trainings, where I helped future ATPs connect with their own angels and guides. It was so exciting to see others experience the wise, loving, and healing messages from their Teams. During that period, I also read many books and took many programs on channeling, connecting with the spiritual world, healing, past life regression, and manifesting your heart's desires.

Now, I have a deeper understanding of my Spiritual Support Team and the ways to connect with its members. What I call my Team is a group of non-physical beings who guide me, help me, and cheer me on. My Team is comprised of angels, archangels (like Archangel Michael), spirit guides, ascended masters (like Jesus), highly evolved beings from other dimensions, deceased loved-ones, my own spirit (my soul or Higher Self), and Source (God). Most of the time I address them as a group, and sometimes I address one of them in particular.

We all have a Spiritual Support Team. It doesn't matter what our spiritual beliefs are: our Team is there to help us in our daily lives. And we can all learn to connect with this source of inner guidance for clarity and assistance.

I love helping people connect with their inner guidance and their own Teams. Together with our Teams, I remind others of their divine identities and help them to discover their soul's purpose, to find their passion, and live their greatest destiny. Through my work, I share the tools and strategies I've gained, both from my Team's insights and from my personal experience. This is my play, purpose, and passion! And I feel honored and blessed to be able to do this.

***

When I realized that Matt and I were struggling—and then, that divorce might be the best choice—it was hard to make sense of it. In many ways, I felt like an empowered, connected woman. I felt like I had so much insight from my own intuition and my Team: why couldn't I use it to improve my marriage? Why was I still struggling?

With my Team's insights, I began to see the journey of my divorce as a gift—and in retrospect, I saw that the painful experiences I had were part of my soul's path towards remembering, reconnecting with, and expressing my True Self.

What follows is the story of my journey of empowerment through self-love. It is my personal diary, where I share in intimate detail my passage through my life's darkest period...when my marriage fell apart...and how my Team helped me through it. At the beginning of my journey, my Team guided me to write down my thoughts, feelings, and experiences, and these are the entries I share with you here.

My divorce journey takes you through each of the seven phases I went through.

I was:

D errailed: I felt confused and lost. Then, I was

I solated: I felt alone and disconnected. Next, I felt like a

V ictim: I perceived myself to be powerless. I was

O verwhelmed: it was too much to handle, emotionally and physically. But then, I

R efocused on loving myself, and I gained clarity. As I felt better, I became

C entered: I was connected to my soul and my highest vision. Finally, I was

E mpowered: I experienced the power of Love within me creating a version of me that is wise, happy, and confident.

And I got to experience the life of my dreams unfolding before me.

Derailed, Isolated, Victim, Overwhelmed, Refocused, Centered, and finally, Empowered. You get to walk with me from the moment I felt Derailed in realizing something was not right in my marriage, to finally feeling Empowered and free to be me!

My journey was not always a direct one. For example, as I progressed through the seven stages of divorce, I sometimes found myself feeling Overwhelmed—I would Refocus, love myself, and feel better...only to feel Overwhelmed again after a challenging experience. In retrospect, I see that my journey looked more like an upward spiral: I sometimes took two steps forward and one step back. The chapters in this book trace my upward spiral. As I gained confidence, I knew that each step forwards or backwards was leading me towards my Empowerment.

***

Have you ever felt angry, disillusioned, or fearful in the face of change? If you have...this book is for you. In reading my story, you'll see how I dealt with these all-too-human emotions to later transform them into compassion, peace and empowerment through self-love.

During the phases of my journey, I experienced self-doubt, sorrow, grief, pain, and loss of identity. I felt like my foundation was crumbling beneath me. But with the help of my Team's insights, I transformed my perspective, and began to feel self-confident, happy, whole, healed, connected, supported, hopeful, empowered, bright, seen, heard, loved, worthy, beautiful, smart, and wise. In this sense, my divorce was the best thing that ever happened to me.

While my journey was unique, the lessons I learned are universal—they can help you through your own divorce or its aftermath, or through any difficult transition you might be facing.

In these chapters, I share the lessons that helped me grow and empower myself. The most important of these lessons was to love myself!

My Team reminds me often...*When Love Appears, Fear Disappears.* The key to my empowerment was to love myself.

When I started doing so, the fears of not being liked or loved, not being good enough, not able to support myself financially, being on my own, being alone or disconnected, and many others, all disappeared.

Love is truly the answer...and now I *know* that I Am Love.

My divorce is the greatest gift I have received. It connected me back to my True Self: the divine, empowered, joyful, wise, and playful me!

Are you ready to take your own journey towards Love? This book is my gift to you.

Chapter 1: Derailed

"It's OK to get lost once in a while.
It's sometimes by getting lost
that we find ourselves."

—Robert Tew

I signed up to run the Tough Mudder, a military-style obstacle course, in May of 2015. I was excited to do it with Matt: together, we would build the endurance to run through the mud and get messy. We'd tackle obstacles together—just as we did every day in raising our two boys. And we'd have fun.

I never anticipated the obstacles I would face before I stepped foot on the course.

I became aware that something wasn't quite right in my marriage in July. It took me by surprise: I had just experienced the best few months in my relationship with my husband in a long time. We were playful with each other, we went out on a few dates, and I felt emotionally connected to him. I was so happy!

I remember back at the beginning of this year, in January, I was sitting at my kitchen counter with my New Year's goal-setting workbook in front of me. As I went through the questions of what I wanted this new year to be like, I told the universe, God, and my Spiritual Support Team:

"I want this year to be the best year of my life! I am ready and committed to make it happen. Thank you for helping me create the best life possible for myself in all areas of my life: my relationships (especially my marriage), my work, my finances, my body, and my spiritual connection."

I wrote several pages with all the details of what I wanted each of those areas to look like...and most importantly, how awesome I would feel.

I thought everything would get better from that moment on. I felt like I was on a roll! I was feeling so excited about my life, but little did I know what would start happening soon after.

During this period, I asked my Team for help with the Tough Mudder, and I received wonderful insights. However, I did not ask them for their wisdom to help me with my relationship until later. During the beginning stages of feeling so lost and confused in my marriage, I didn't think to ask them for clarity. Maybe I was so unclear that confusion clouded me from thinking to ask for divine help…or maybe I was afraid of what I would hear. When it came to my marriage, I had been **Derailed.**

***

7/18/15: I am feeling uneasy. Something's not right. Matt has not been acting like himself lately. Ever since he went out with his guy friends to Tony's lake house a couple of weeks ago, I can sense tension coming from him. Maybe he's stressed out about finances. He did mention we lost a lot of money in our retirement account when the market got hit recently. Or maybe it's work. He works so hard and such long hours. He's always working. Maybe he needs more space. I wish he would talk to me. I want to help him feel better. I am not sure what to do.

7/30/15: I am feeling confused. Matt has been distancing himself from me. He's acting cold. No more affection. No lightness. No playfulness. I hate feeling disconnected from him! He's been going out with the guys more than usual, spending more money at restaurants and bars, and coming home later than he used to. When I asked him about it last week, he got really upset. I found it strange that he would swear at me for asking him where he was and why he wouldn't return my texts or calls that night. This is the first time in the 23 years we've been together that he's sworn at me. I hate the tension between us. I hate it so much that I found myself apologizing to him for asking him too many questions.

Yesterday was my birthday. He forgot, even after I reminded him a couple of times during the week. He must be very stressed at work. Today, when I told him he'd forgotten, he apologized and said he had a lot going on. I told him I understood and I didn't make a big deal out of it. I wonder what's going on.

8/21/15: I've been keeping myself busy at home and with the boys. Summer vacation will be ending soon, so we are getting ready for school to start. We've been getting school supplies and clothes. Matt's recent unusual behavior has continued. I wish I could easily talk to him about what is bothering him, but communicating openly has never been our strong area. I am feeling disconnected, unclear, and a little lost.

Just a few months ago, between April and July, we were having a good time. It was the best spring and summer together in a long time! He seemed playful and light. Our dates made me feel special. I don't know what's going on now. I don't remember anything specific that happened that would have resulted in this change in behavior. I have an empty feeling inside my heart. I am lonely, and I am sad. My light is getting dimmer.

9/19/15: Matt has been going out almost every weeknight in the last couple of months. He's coming home between 8:45 and 10:30 p.m., and sometimes as late as 2 a.m. He is with his guy friends. I feel jealous of them: I wish it were me he was going out with after work. I long to have my friend and husband back. Where did he go? I miss our time together. I miss our light-hearted conversations. I miss his touch. I am so sad. It seems he doesn't want to be with me. Sometimes he gets home and doesn't even say hello or look at me. He greets our boys and then ignores me. It is so strange. I don't understand, especially since I always make it a point to greet him happily with a smile. What did I do? I have no idea.

I don't think I am the problem. It can't be me. I feel I am such a good wife! I always appreciate him for everything he does, especially how he provides for us. I am always positive, smiling, and interested in what he says. I make sure everything in the house is taken care of so that he comes home to a peaceful and beautiful space. I also give him a lot of freedom to do what he enjoys—from riding his bike to going out with the guys.

I feel I am an awesome mom, too. I dedicate my life to our boys, making sure they have everything they need. That they are happy and taken care of. There is always a home-cooked meal ready for them and clean laundry available. I give them anything they need. I am always driving them everywhere, too. I easily spend over two hours going to and from school and to their extracurricular activities every day. My boys are my light! I'd do anything for them.

***

As my marriage became harder, I didn't know what to think of the other obstacle course I'd agreed to face: the Tough Mudder. Feeling lost and alone, was it really the right time to run through the mud? So much went through my head:

"I can't believe I signed up for this!"
"I have never liked mud!"
"I don't even garden because I don't like the feeling of dirt on my hands!"
"Will I be able to do this?"
"I'm supposed to go through a 10-mile course, with 20 military-style obstacles, and they ALL involve MUD! This is CRAZY!"
"I am feeling anxious. Am I ready to go through this?"

I asked my Spiritual Support Team for their help in facing this course. This is what I heard:

This event can be an opportunity for you to overcome fears and limiting perspectives in your own life. Look at what mud represents to you. Look at what each obstacle in the Tough Mudder represents in your life. What struggle, challenge, or fear does it represent? Then, as you are going through each obstacle at the event, see yourself tackling and conquering your fears.

I thought that was a great idea. I could use this event as an opportunity to grow in my spiritual understanding and to face my deepest fears. I just didn't know what I was going to find...

I got my notebook and pen, along with my computer. I was ready to go deep.
I went to the Tough Mudder website and made a list of each of the obstacles on the course map. I went through the description of each one, watching YouTube videos to get a better idea of what they entailed.

There were 20 obstacles in total. I felt confident that I could do many of them, but several really triggered me.

"Mud...Yuck!" was my first reaction at the thought of mud, and there's a *lot* of mud in this event. I decided to start by finding out why I don't like mud in general, and why I try to avoid it at any cost. I asked, "What does mud represent to me?"

My Team told me: *For you, mud represents difficulties and challenges: struggle, feeling dirty, and discomfort. You see it as the opposite of ease, cleanliness, and organization.*

I thought, "I don't like mud. Yuck! I also don't like to struggle, or to feel dirty or uncomfortable."

My Team told me: *Mud (and all it represents) is just mud. You are the one giving it a negative meaning. This meaning you give it creates your resistance towards it.*
If you see mud as neutral, without judgment, your whole perspective towards mud AND EVERYTHING IT REPRESENTS will shift.

You could give it a different meaning, and even laugh at the mud! Recognize that every challenge (a.k.a. "muddy obstacle") you experience in your life brings a GIFT to you. Every single one! Mud can be your friend!

I knew I was likely to find myself face-down in the mud at some point during the obstacle course. My shoes, my shirt, and my hands would be covered in it—I'd likely find my face in it, too, kissing the mud. What would this kiss mean? I wrote: "To me, the Kiss of Mud obstacle represents getting deep in the mud and being in the middle of challenges and struggle. It feels icky, sticky, yucky, uncomfortable, and maybe even painful."

My Team told me: *Here are some tips to help you go through this obstacle:*

- *Be totally neutral about mud.*
- *Stay focused on your destination.*
- *Keep your head up! It will help you to see the path ahead more clearly.*
- *Shift your perspective about being immersed in mud. Think, "Mud can be fun!" Remember that mud—and challenges—can help you grow and gain wisdom. Lighten up about it!*
- *Choose to enjoy the ride. Enjoy the ups and downs, even if you get really, really dirty and uncomfortable!*

What do you want mud to mean for you? What would be empowering for you? What would make you smile when rolling in mud?

As you go through the Kiss of Mud obstacle, repeat this mantra, "Mud has no meaning. Mud just is. Mud is my friend. Mud is fun!"

I wondered about another event—the King of Swingers. This brought up an even bigger fear.

I would have to jump from a 12-foot high ledge to hopefully catch a swing bar and then let myself go. I would then fall into the mucky waters below me.

This represented my fear of being alone and disconnected, especially while going through something really difficult, like jumping off a cliff. Yikes. But when I asked my Team for insights to help me with this obstacle, I saw an image of angel wings opening up from my back.

My Team told me: *Who You Really Are is Spirit in human form! And your Spirit can fly! See your angel wings opening up behind your back as you are jumping off into the air.*
I began to hear the song lyrics, *"You are the wind beneath my wings..."* in my head.

My Team continued: *God is the wind beneath your wings. You are always connected to Source (God). You are also divinely supported by your Spiritual Support Team, always! There's no moment when you are alone. No moment when you are disconnected. But you will experience yourself as being alone and disconnected if you don't remember this higher Truth. Remember your divine oneness and connection, and you will then experience it.*

With the help of my Team, I was going to face each obstacle with a new perspective. I was ready to face Electroshock Therapy and The Warrior Carry—as well as my own fears.

***

9/25/15: The boys, Matt, and I are leaving to Maine tonight. Tomorrow is the Tough Mudder. Why did I sign up for this event? Oh yes, because I was looking forward to doing it with Matt. Back in May when I brought up the idea of doing this, he said that if I did it, he'd do it, too. I was excited to share this adventure with him. It seemed fun at the time. It would be something we could do together and maybe it would help us connect even more....oh right, AND my Team *strongly* suggested I do it.

Well, we'll see how it goes. I am excited that my friend Loni and her husband are also doing it with us. We are leaving this evening and it starts early tomorrow morning.

9/28/15: Oh wow! What an experience the Tough Mudder was! I am so glad I did it!

***

The guidance from my Team worked.

The mud wasn't so bad. I went through it smiling.

I wasn't planning to do the Artic Enema—a dive into a pool that was freezing and filled with ice cubes.

I thought to myself beforehand: "No thank you! I can't even go in a pool because I don't like the feeling of going into cold water." Plus, I read that the icy water in this event could be so cold that your muscles go into shock. They won't move. Even when your mind says, "move," your body can have a hard time obeying. My thoughts continued: "I am not doing this one. I don't even have to ask what the lesson is on this one. I know: the lesson is that I don't have to go through unnecessary trauma. I can choose to NOT do it!"

But on that day in September, my perspective changed.

Somehow, I found myself in line with others going on this obstacle. "How did I get here? I am not supposed to be here," I told myself, but with my husband and teammate friends looking forward to it, laughing and excited about it, I suddenly felt a surge of confidence that surpassed my nervousness. "I'll do it!" I said to myself.

Before I knew it, there I was...going fast down the steep slide into the freezing, ice-cold water...I was completely submerged...

"Holy shit! This water is freaking cold. I am under water. I can't open my eyes in this mucky water. How do I stand up?" I then felt someone lift me up so that I could stand. Matt, my knight in shining armor, came to my rescue. I was SO grateful.

I survived that obstacle.

Later, I received the following message from my Team about what happened to me:

It is wise to choose not to go through unnecessary trauma, and still sometimes, you will find yourself in the middle of it. Know that even in the direst of experiences, you are never alone. You are always supported by seen and unseen friends!

In the Warrior Carry obstacle, you are supposed to carry your partner for 50 yards, and then switch. This was the most fun event for me. I felt so strong carrying my husband for 50 yards.

He was super funny, pretending he was a knight and I was his horse. Hmmm...good thing we got to switch. I laughed so hard. And it was not as difficult as I thought it would be.

I am stronger than I thought I was.

I had wondered: "I think this one will be fun, but am I strong enough to carry Matt? Will he get tired of carrying me? Will I be too heavy for him?"

My Team told me: *Sometimes, you are meant to carry others in life, just for a moment to help them out...and other times, they are meant to carry you. You are each other's support. Believe in yourself. Know that you ARE strong enough, wise enough, and resourceful enough to help others. At the same time, be gracious in accepting others' help. You don't have to carry the load all the time. Allow yourself to be carried. Accept and welcome heaven's help, in all ways, including human help.*

I even made it through my fear of pain, made manifest in the last obstacle, Electroshock Therapy, where there are live hanging wires that will shock you with electricity. Not all of them will shock you, but some will. I wondered—would it hurt? How much?

At the event, I found myself thinking, "I am standing in front of the wires. I am going for it. OK, here I go…Cool! I am almost at the end of the wire-filled path without being shocked. I think I may be able to avoid being shocked. This could be really eeeeeasy…O-O-U-U-U-C-H. THAT HURT! I got shocked. I am about to fall in the mud because my knees are buckling underneath me. Almost fell…but I made it."

Being shocked was debilitating. My knees gave in. I almost fell on the muddy track, but I was able to regain my balance, and I got to the end without falling.
I made it. I did it. I finished the Tough Mudder.

At the end, I was smiling. All I felt was a huge sense of accomplishment and pride. The Tough Mudder…what a gift!

This is what I learned:

- Mud (and everything it represents to me) has no meaning.
- I give mud (and challenge) its meaning.
- Mud is my friend.

- I am divinely connected, supported, and loved through it all.
- How I see mud (and everything in life) is my choice.

I learned to look at mud—and challenges—differently:

My OLD meaning for M.U.D. –> **M**ost. **U**ncomfortable. **D**oing.
My NEW meaning for M.U.D. –> **M**ost. **U**plifting. **D**iscovery.

***

10/21/15: I love my Team! Their messages are always so loving and wise! I *feel* the deep truth within their words. Their messages always make me feel loved and at peace. They are always encouraging me to believe in myself. I feel they are my greatest cheerleaders. I should talk to them more often. I feel truly blessed that I have this beautiful relationship with them, and that I can hear them. I remember it wasn't always like this, but I am really glad I can talk with them in this way now.

***

Although my relationship with my husband was more difficult than ever, my relationship with my Team was changing and growing. I learned so much from them at this time.

Your life is like the Tough Mudder, my Spiritual Support Team told me.

"What do you mean?" I replied. My Team answered, and their answers changed my perspective on life.

The Tough Mudder event you just went through is like having a physical life on Earth. There are many similarities between the two. Becoming aware of these similarities can help you see your life from a different perspective...a perspective that is insightful, empowering, and more freeing!

"OK," *I said.* "I want to hear this perspective. Tell me how life on Earth is like the Tough Mudder?"

1. You Enter It by Choice

You made the choice to sign up for the Tough Mudder, right? You also chose the time and place you would do it. Likewise, your spirit chooses to come to Earth to have a physical life. You, as your True Self, chose when and where you would come to Earth as you.

2. You Choose a Team

When you joined the Tough Mudder, you got to choose a team to support you and share the experience. Your team members may be with you throughout the event or only for parts of it. In life, you also choose your team. You choose your parents, your best friends, your partners, and even those who bring about conflict.

3. You Interact with Other Teams

During the Tough Mudder, you help others and others help you. Sometimes you consciously choose how you will interact with them, and other times, it just happens. The same occurs with the people in your life.

4. There are Challenges

In both journeys, there are going to be challenges, obstacles, and "mud." Remember that these experiences are all part of the journey, offering opportunities for growth, clarity, and gifts.

5. There are Beautiful Experiences

Your life offers you beautiful experiences filled with joy, laughter, excitement, support, love, adventures, beauty, fulfillment, well-being, and peace! These experiences make it easy to open your heart and experience your True Self: that magnificent being of joy and light that you are in truth.

6. You are Supported Every Step of the Way

Throughout your experiences, you have lots of support from seen and unseen forces and friends. Sometimes you are aware of this support, and other times you are not. Asking for help and welcoming it makes it easier for you to experience this support.

7. You Always Have a Choice

You always have a choice about the path you take and how to take it. You choose which obstacles you tackle and how, which ones you want to skip, etc. You get to decide what is best for you, depending on the resources, conditions, and intentions you and your soul have at the moment.

8. It's About the Journey, Not the Destination

You signed up for both events to experience the JOURNEY...with its ups and downs, co-creative interactions, emotions, and many opportunities to express who you are. You did not sign up to get to the destination. Your destination, as a spirit, is already guaranteed: you go back Home, to the non-physical.

Many people think it's the destination, getting to "heaven," that is the goal. The truth is that your spirit is thrilled to be on Earth! Heaven is not a destination; it is within you and all around you. Having a lifetime on Earth is truly a heavenly gift.

9. Your Perspective Determines Your Experience

How you experience your journey will be determined by your perspective. If you see your journey as difficult and feel fear, doubt, and worry—you WILL EXPERIENCE THAT.

On the other hand, if you approach life with a sense of excitement and confidence, anticipating support and that things will work out for you, you WILL EXPERIENCE THAT. Your life will be easier, more supportive, and more joyful. You will find that life supports you every step of the way, even when challenges appear.

10. You Can Do It Again!

The finish line is a temporary destination. When your physical life "ends," your life still goes on, but now you have a new level of awareness and an awesome feeling of accomplishment. You gained much wisdom and insight throughout your lifetime, and you may decide to do it again.

"Why?" you may ask. The answer is simple: for the JOY of it. You may find joy in gaining a new level of mastery in a specific subject, or taking a different approach in some of the events and challenges life on Earth offers, or maybe the joy of being of service to others...and always, always, for the joy of EXPRESSING your magnificent Self, your divine Spirit.

The PURPOSE of life is Joy. The purpose of YOUR Life is to express yourself in whatever way gives you Joy!

The BASIS of life is Freedom. You get to choose what you experience, even limitation. You may not always choose consciously, but you are always choosing nonetheless with your thoughts and vibration.

The NATURAL RESULT of life is Growth. You continue to grow and evolve, no matter what you do.

YOU are a beautiful gift to the world. You are Love. You are loved.

"Thank you, guys," I said. "You are the BEST."

***

My relationship with my Team was stronger than ever. I felt so clear on the purpose of challenges in life: I was ready to overcome them.

So why weren't things between Matt and me working?

As soon as I got back home from this life-changing event, I felt Derailed again. I couldn't find my way within my relationship. I felt lost.

***

10/31/15: Tonight was Halloween. The boys went out trick-or-treating with their friends. I was looking forward to spending some time alone with Matt before the boys came back, but my hopes quickly evaporated when he got home. Instead of coming to the living room, where I told him I was, he went straight to the den without even coming in to say, "Hi."

As he headed upstairs, I thought, "Wow, am I not even important enough to him for him to come over to see me and say hi? This hurts so much." After wiping off my tears, I went upstairs to the den. There he was, at his computer, like he usually is until late at night—when he's home. I tried making light conversation, but was quickly shut down when he got upset that I asked about what he was looking at. My heart ached. I left...and cried...again.

***

I was derailed. But later, I gained insights from my Team.

***

Divine Insights from my Team

*You were **Derailed**. You felt lost and confused. The main reason you felt derailed was because you lost yourself in your marriage. You could say that you forgot Who You Really Are within the context of your family.*

You forgot that you are the source of love and everything else you need. You made your husband your source of love. So when he stopped "loving" you, you felt lost, unstable, and nervous.

You also did not value, honor, or respect yourself, even when you thought you did. Therefore, you did not truly love yourself. You mistakenly believed that to be a "good and loving" wife and mother, you needed to put your husband and children's needs, wants, and opinions before yours. You sacrificed yourself for them. This is not true love. True love starts with loving yourself.

When you do not honor yourself or your needs, you are forsaking yourself. This is the highest form of betrayal...betrayal of Self. You are forsaking the divine within you.

The universe is set up to mirror your thoughts about life and about yourself. If you are betraying yourself with your thoughts, words or actions, you will find yourself being betrayed by others. This is a gift from the universe: when you realize what is happening, you can choose differently. This is what happened to you during the beginning of your divorce journey.

Chapter 2: Isolated

"You cannot be lonely if
you like the person you are alone with."

—Wayne Dyer

As summer ended, my feeling of Derailment changed: now, I felt **Isolated.** My husband remained distant, and I still didn't know what had happened, or what I could do to improve things.

I kept appreciating Matt for his support and his actions, and continued being as positive and light in my demeanor as I could. I kept taking care of the house, and cooking, cleaning, and caring for our boys. It didn't seem to make a difference. Sometimes he would give me a small compliment. "Dinner was good," he might say—when he actually had dinner at home on the weekends. It was rare he'd eat dinner with us at home during the week.

I felt alone in our marriage, and even in our home. We had been sleeping in different rooms for over three years because he said he could not sleep with me snoring. I had offered to sleep in a different bedroom so that he could get a good night's sleep. He gladly accepted. Once again, I felt rejected and abandoned. But even though it bothered me, I didn't tell him that I needed more connection and physical affection in other ways to make up for the lack of connection sleeping together offered me.

At first, I didn't know where to turn for help. But soon, guidance came.

***

11/6/15: I can't take this anymore...the late nights away with his friends...the lack of connection...the emotional distance between us. I feel so alone. I cried so much last night. I cried myself to sleep...again. All through the night I prayed. I meditated. I wrote a note to him at 2 a.m., but I don't think I'll give it to him. I am afraid of what might happen as a result. Instead, I am focusing on the positive parts of our relationship, his positive qualities, and what is working in my life. This makes me feel better and gives me hope again. This is what I wrote:

> Dear Matt, I need and long for your loving affection. I need and long for your caring words, your loving look, and your warm touch. I feel abandoned, physically and emotionally. I feel vulnerable and unsafe. I can't be in a relationship with neither intimacy nor expressions of love. I am trying to figure out how to find our connection. I know it's there: we experienced it last summer. I don't want to have my heart crushed. I just want to be happy. I want you to be happy. I want *us* to be happy. Our family's wellbeing depends on it. I am trying to figure out how to be happy without your physical affection and expressions of love, but is that even fair? How can I be in a relationship where I don't feel loved? What do you need from me?

11/8/15: I feel a part of me is slowly dying. Without feeling physically and emotionally connected to the person I love most, my soul is starving…for love.

11/10/15: I wonder what I did. Why is he acting this way when all I have done is be nice? Maybe I have been *too* nice. I feel like I am being punished for something...and I don't even know what it is.

11/11/15: I got this in my inbox today. It's an email from Neale Donald Walsch, the author of *Conversations with God* and one of my favorite inspirational authors. This message caught my eye and I felt it was speaking directly to me:

> On this day of your life,
> Dear Friend, I believe God wants you to know...
>
> ...that the goodness in your life does not come to you from someone else. When you see this, you will be free.
>
> There is no reason and no need to "play up" to another, or to try to remain in good graces. Remain in your own, by not betraying yourself. Simply speak your truth, with gentleness and love.
>
> And have the courage, for what you seek is not outside of you. It is not a gift from another person. It is yours—

to give, not to acquire. Let no one, therefore, hold you hostage. Not your partner, not your boss, not your family...and certainly not your God.

You know exactly why you received this message today.

Today, my Team suggested I start journaling what I've been going through, what is happening in my relationship, how I feel, and the insights I have through the process. They said that doing this would help me gain clarity, heal, and help others in the future. I like the idea.

11/15/15: I mustered the courage to talk to Matt tonight. I couldn't take it anymore. I needed to know what was going on and let him know that whatever he was going through, I was there for him. I waited for a time when the boys would be busy in their rooms and I went to Matt's bedroom to talk with him.

"I need to talk to you. Is this a good time?" I asked. "Sure," he said, so I continued. "My intention is to relieve the pressure, not to add to it. This is my perspective and I want to hear your perspective, too. You've been working so hard and for such long hours lately. You've always worked so hard to provide for us. You've been amazing. You've provided so much, financially and in so many other ways, for the boys and for me.

I love you for this. It's just that I've noticed that there's something different now. I sense you don't want to work so hard. You don't seem as happy. You look more stressed. We barely see each other and you've distanced yourself from me. You are not your happy, playful, and warm self anymore.

I wonder if it's worth it. Is working so hard worth your happiness? I want you to be happy. I want *us* to be happy. I want to feel connected to you. If you want to do something different for work, know that I support you. You have so many positive qualities that would make you an asset to others. Know that I support you no matter what you do. I just want us to be happy. What do *you* want?"

I was shocked at his reply as he smirked, "Work is fine and getting better. I don't know what you are talking about me distancing myself from you. Maybe the reason is *you*. We can't see eye to eye on how to parent the boys."

What? Me? Parenting? This didn't make any sense! I couldn't believe this.

"Did you just hear what I said?" I replied. "I want to support you and I am asking you how I can do that. I want you to be happy. I want *us* to be happy, and all you tell me is that it's *my* fault because of the way I parent?"

He said nothing. He did nothing. No response. He just stared at the floor. Nothing more: I was devastated. He was done talking, and I couldn't say anything else. I had a knot in my throat. My heart ached. I didn't know what else to do but leave his room.

11/19/15: I've cried for three days straight after our last conversation. There've been piles of dirty, wet tissues next to my bed each night, and next to the living room couch during the day. I haven't been able to hold back the tears. They just keep flowing. I am trying my best not to cry in front of the boys, but sometimes I can't help it. I am doing the best I can, yet I really don't know what to do. I feel my life force is being sucked out of me. I feel weak.

11/30/15: This past weekend was Thanksgiving. We just came back from my mother-in-law's house in Maine. We celebrated Thanksgiving weekend there with Matt's family, like we usually do. I love my mother-in-law. She is like a mother to me and she treats me like a dear daughter. She always has, and for that I am so grateful, especially when I don't have any family nearby.

This year, my mom came from Florida to join us, but even though I had so many people there whom I love and who love me, I couldn't help but feel isolated and alone. I kept feeling ignored by Matt. He walked way in front of me at the city's Christmas tree lighting, as if not wanting me to be next to him. What I would have done for him to hold my hand. He'd come into the house saying hello to everyone except me, totally ignoring my presence in the room. So much love around me…and still, I felt so alone. It was the saddest Thanksgiving I've ever experienced.

12/3/15: I decided to work with a relationship coach. I'm starting this week. I've been studying Alison Armstrong's materials for many years now. I love her "Understanding Men" and "The Queen's Code" programs. I've found them very helpful, at least personally, in my understanding of the differences between men and women and what makes a relationship work. I feel I now need personal help from an expert to implement these insights in my relationship.

12/5/15: I told Matt I was learning ways to communicate more easily and clearly with him, and asked him if he wanted to do it together. Unfortunately, he was not that open to it. He said that if I found something helpful, I could tell him what I learned. How can I do this alone? It takes two, doesn't it?

12/15/15: He rejected me again. He's rejected me every single time I've initiated being intimate for months. I can barely stand the pain of this rejection. I feel abandoned and betrayed by the person I thought was my best friend—the man who I adored, trusted, and dedicated my life to. This empty feeling within my heart is unbearable. It feels like my best friend has stabbed me from the back, right in my heart.

I feel so alone and disconnected. My soul thrives on connection! I can't bear this empty feeling. I feel unsafe. I am afraid.

12/20/16: I'm starting to notice that I am getting emails in my inbox with messages that I feel are speaking to me. I wonder if they are divinely inspired messages from my Team. It feels like they are. Today I got an email from Paul Ferrini, author of *Love Without Conditions* and many other books on love, healing, and forgiveness. It read:

"Taking Back What You Gave Away"

You won't experience true intimacy
If you spend your life trying to please others.

One who gives herself away
Will have to take herself back sooner or later.

One who says "yes" because she is afraid to say "no"
Will say "no" in the end, but it will not be
A gentle, compassionate "no."

It will be harsh, unforgiving "no"
Of one trying to survive, of one afraid of suffocating.

It will be the cry of one who feels betrayed,
Although in truth she has betrayed herself.

***

Shortly after, I received another e-mail from Neale Donald Walsch that spoke directly to me. It read:

> On this day of your life,
> Dear Friend, I believe God wants you to know...
>
> ...that it is okay to be at a place of struggle.
> Struggle is just another word for growth.
>
> Even the most evolved beings find themselves in a place
> of struggle now and then. In fact, struggle is a sure sign
> to them that they are expanding; it is their indication of
> real and important progress.

> The only one who doesn't struggle is the one
> who
> doesn't grow. So if you are struggling right now,
> see it as
> a terrific sign -- and *celebrate* your struggle.

Through these e-mails, I felt my Team telling me that I was going through a struggle because I was growing. Even though it was hard for me to see, I could feel that this was true.

***

12/23/15: I've been trying to protect the boys from the tension in the house and from the pain I've been feeling. I try to keep them from noticing how sad I am, but sometimes, the tears just run down my face and I can't hold them back. The tears come when I least expect them...driving them to school, at gymnastics or hockey, while cooking dinner, doing the dishes, while at the kitchen counter helping them with homework at night...

***

I've always loved caring for my two boys. But during this period, it was overwhelming to have so much to do, and to feel so isolated. I spent so much time doing special things for the boys: I took long drives to bring John to his hockey practices across the border in Massachusetts, and I cooked special foods for Alex to support his athletic performance in gymnastics.

The few times I expressed overwhelm to Matt, he didn't seem to have any sympathy. On the contrary, he'd say that the kids were always first and that I was being selfish for not wanting to do what was best for them.

I wished he would be my partner: that he would be there to listen to how I was feeling and offer his support.

He never seemed to show any signs that he cared about how I felt. If I was sad or upset, he never asked me if I was OK. He never said, "I'm sorry" for hurting my feelings. It was always me who kept apologizing or trying to see things from his perspective.

How could I start feeling better without his help?

***

1/1/16: Happy New Year, Dumari! I love you.

1/7/16: I am so excited! Dad is coming tomorrow to visit me all the way from Puerto Rico! I haven't seen him in almost two years. I adore my dad. My parents have been divorced since I was two years old, but I've always had a beautiful relationship with my dad. To me, he's not only my dad, but also my friend and wise guide.

1/12/16: It was so wonderful having Dad here. We talked for hours. He wanted to know what was going on in my life. I told him. He listened with an open mind and an open heart. I loved that he never took sides. He would try putting himself in Matt's shoes to help me understand where Matt may be coming from. One of Dad's many talents is that he's a professional mediator, so I am sure that experience helped in this situation. Plus, my dad has been through three divorces himself, so he's had some experience in that area. LOL!

Dad told me that during his visit, he noticed how my energy shifted as soon as Matt came in our home. He said my energy shrunk, my light got dimmer, and that I became like a little puppy asking for love. I was stunned when I heard that. I thought I had already done so much work in that area, but apparently there was still much more to do. Hearing my perceptive dad tell me this made a big impact on me.

Dad told me it was important for me to reflect back on when I felt I started changing who I really was within my relationship with Matt. I thought about it and two memories came to mind, both over 20 years ago when we were first dating.

In the first scene, it was a hot summer day when we were both in college. We were going to the mall and we were in the parking lot walking towards the shopping mall. I was wearing a short shirt that showed my belly, just like what I wore back in Puerto Rico. Two guys walked by and looked at my abs. Matt looked at me and said that I should not be wearing clothes that showed my skin like that because it made men look at me and get the wrong impression. I said that this was the way women dressed in Puerto Rico and that it had nothing to do with wanting to be provocative. Plus, he should be proud of showing me off because I was with *him*. "You are not in Puerto Rico. You are in New England, and things here are different," he said. I felt that he was trying to protect me, so even though I defended the way I dressed at that moment, I started changing the way I dressed to fit in and be more conservative.

The second scene flashed in my mind's eye…we were in his apartment and I mentioned to him that even though I was raised Catholic, I would not label myself that way anymore because some of my spiritual beliefs had shifted. I said I didn't think Catholics would call me a Catholic, but that I didn't think the label really mattered because I felt my spiritual connection was strong.

I said this was a good opportunity to talk about our spiritual beliefs in an open way and to get to know what was important to each one of us in that area. I wanted to talk about life and what we valued. He got upset at my statement that I didn't think I was Catholic. He did not want to talk about it, and left the room. I followed him, saying that I was really interested in what he thought and that I wanted to share my thoughts, too. That talking about it would be good for us. I was left alone, feeling unheard and misunderstood. I felt judged for my beliefs, and not important enough for my thoughts and opinions to matter.

This happened so many times while we were together, especially when we dated and during the first several years of our marriage. I would want to talk about something. He did not because it upset him. He would leave the room. I'd followed him. He would not talk. I'd leave, go to the bathroom, and cry.

I've cried so much while in this relationship for different reasons, but mostly because of feeling judged, criticized, not valued, not heard, not seen, and ultimately, not loved.

Not everything was difficult in our relationship, though. There were also good experiences and times when there was lightness, laughter, playfulness, and connection. There were also many things I felt very grateful for. One of them was that I was able to dedicate my time to two of my most favorite things in the whole world: my boys and my light work.

I really love being a mom. I love being home for the kids and making sure they have a beautiful, peaceful place to be. I get to be with them all the time and be available for them whenever they need me. I've also been able to volunteer a lot at their school and be very involved in their lives, which I absolutely love.

I also LOVE my work. Even though I don't get to spend that much time on it because my family comes first to me, I feel so good helping others connect with their inner guidance and Spiritual Support Teams. I love the positive impact our Spiritual Support Teams' messages have on my clients! I can see how healing and empowering it is for them. It lights them up, and it lights me up. It truly makes my heart sing.

I am grateful that Matt provides me with financial support and takes care of the boys while I need to do things that are related to my work. Even though he isn't really interested in what I do, doesn't want me to talk about it with him, and won't even look at my website, he does support me so that I can do what I love.

After I shared all this with Dad, he said to me, *"First, I feel sad that I had never noticed before how you changed when Matt was around. Your light gets dim and your energy feels so small. Second, it's really important that you reconnect with the true Dumari, the Dumari before Matt. The Dumari who was joyful, carefree, playful and light, the Dumari who was sexy, and who loved to dance!*

"You've got to reconnect with your roots. Let's listen to some good Latin songs on Pandora and watch YouTube videos. Listen to them often, and most importantly, DANCE to these songs! It will help you reconnect. Dance in the kitchen, in the living room,

in your bedroom, wherever. You loved to dance! Just dance and let the music help you reconnect with yourself.

"Let's also look at some specific times when you feel small or disempowered in the relationship, and how to shift that from now on. Let's practice what you would say, what you would do, and how you would feel as the empowered, joyful, bright Dumari that is you."

I feel Dad is an earth angel who was sent to me at the perfect time to help me. He helped me to start reconnecting with the Dumari I had so long forgotten about. I really love to dance...and I had stopped dancing. I love listening to Salsa and Latin music...and I stopped doing so. My dad helped me realize that the Dumari he knew was lost, and he helped me reconnect with her. It felt good to do so. Thank you, Dad!

***

Divine Insights from my Team

***Isolated**. Lonely. Cut off from love. This is how you felt. Yet this is not your Truth. You are never alone! You are never* *separate from Love! However, you will experience yourself as separate from it when you forget your divine identity.*

You are an individualized expression of divinity, of God and Love itself, in human form. When you forget this, you see and experience yourself as separate from everything: from God, from Love, and from others.

Your heart ached because your soul was telling you your perception of separation was not true. It was letting you know that you were looking for Love in the wrong places...outside of you. Love is truly within you. Remember this, and you will feel your Oneness with All. You will know you are whole and complete, connected, and never, ever alone. You will fall in love with yourself and you will know yourself as the source of the Love you seek.

It is nobody's job to fill the void between you and your True Self. Only you can do that. When you fill that void, you will feel complete, whole, and infinitely connected. The way you start filling that void is by accepting, appreciating, valuing, and honoring yourself in the most loving way you can.

Chapter 3: Victim

"When you realize how perfect everything is,
you will tilt your head back and laugh at the sky."

—Buddha

My feeling of isolation was made worse by my belief that I was a **Victim** in my relationship and had no control over my circumstances. Even though I felt empowered and confident in other areas of my life, in my marriage, I felt helpless.

Growing up, I sometimes felt annoyed at my mother when she played the victim. Although I love and admire her, I didn't want to follow in her footsteps on that path. But during the Thanksgiving when Matt was so distant, I began to realize that I, too, felt like a victim within my marriage. Worse, I had believed that only he had the power to make me feel loved and worthy.

I had always known that the women in my family felt themselves to be less important than the men around them. This belief had been passed down in my family—as in so many other families—for generations and generations. I knew this intellectually, but I didn't realize it played out in my marriage, and even in my relationship with my two sons. When I realized how much this affected me—how it made me feel disempowered—I knew something needed to change.

I needed to let go of my own limiting beliefs if I wanted to stop feeling like a victim. I knew I would have to consciously shift each one of those beliefs. I was the only person who could free me from my victim mentality; I was the only person who could help me feel completely loved.

***

12/3/15: My mom just left after visiting me from Florida for Thanksgiving.
I am so grateful for what happened while she was here. I am thankful for her, and for the beautiful, deep healing I experienced thanks to her.

For most of my life I've struggled with some of my mom's behaviors. Mostly because it has always bothered me how she feels lesser than others and puts everybody else before herself. She has a heart of gold, but she often feels other people are smarter and more important than she is.

She doesn't value herself or her needs, and she sometimes takes the role of the victim. It bothers me! I am constantly telling her to value herself more, to love herself more: that she is more powerful than she realizes, and that she IS the most important person in her life.

I have done much healing work on my feelings towards my mom throughout the years, but I noticed that when she arrived at the airport, I was incredibly triggered by her. Her mere presence annoyed me. Why? I asked myself. She is such a beautiful, loving person. I love her and she loves me so much. What is it that bothers me about my mom? The answer came to me that night as I was falling asleep.

Clarity hit me like a ton of bricks. As I was lying in bed, I heard my Team say,

What bothers you about your mom is that she does not value herself, she gives herself up for others, she doesn't think she is important enough, and she believes everybody else's problems and needs are more important than hers. Your mom is reflecting back to you your own shadows, the parts of YOU that you judge and deny. She is your mirror, to some extent, because even though you don't do this with others, this is what you do with Matt and your boys.

Oh my God! I hadn't seen it before, but they were right. I could see it very clearly now. They continued saying,

Now, remember that Love is the greatest healer, so love her AND love yourself. Love your shadows. Love the parts of her and of yourself that you do not like. Doing this will heal you once and for all. Once you do this, you'll fulfill the main reason you chose her to be your mother in this lifetime.

Wow. This message really hit me at my core. I felt it deeply: my heart opened with a feeling of profound compassion, both for my mom AND for myself. For the next few days, every time I looked at her and felt triggered or annoyed, I said in my mind, "Mami, I love you. I accept ALL of you. Dumari, I love you. I accept ALL of you."

As I did this, I would feel an energetic shift. After doing it for a few days, I felt the healing was complete. I felt healed at the core of my being. It was permanent. And not only did I receive the gift of this healing, I felt that my mom on some level received it too. At that moment, I felt so thankful towards her and her reflection of the parts of me that were asking to be healed with the power of Love.

This was yet another layer peeled off in my journey of empowerment through love. I, once again, chose to love and value myself, and to empower myself fully and completely. I am breaking the cycle I have been carrying on for generations. As I understood this at a deeper level, I intuitively felt I was also energetically helping other women who had been carrying this burden to free themselves.

12/10/15: I was texting with my friend Loni today, sharing my latest updates and feelings. Loni is also very intuitive and can easily hear our Teams' messages. She said Jesus was there with her and he had a message for me. This is what Jesus said to me (through her as we were texting):

Walk with me and see it through my eyes, Dumari. So much pain in both of you (Matt and yourself). Love is the answer you seek, but if there is no love to give, then what do you have to gain, child, but emptiness and sorrow and pity? You are of my kin. We feel much deeper. Hurt much deeper. Our soul seeks nothing but the highest truth. And now I am asking you to see your truth, Dumari. What will the love you seek look like? Feel like? Taste like? Love is the answer.

Thank you, Jesus, for this message. Thank you for helping me see the truth more clearly. Your words are like a healing balm to my wounded heart. Please help me understand what true love really looks like, feels like, and tastes like.

12/15/15: Today, just a couple of weeks after the profound healing I experienced with my mom, I was talking to my friend Swati. She mentioned that ever since she's known me (about 13 years), she's noticed that I felt lesser than my husband and my boys.

When I asked her why she thought that, she said, "Because you always put them first. You always want to please them, and even change the way you really are in order to do so. I see you being this bright light, so joyful and beautiful. Even other people tell me that about you. But when you are with your boys and husband, you shift."

I argued with her that that was not true. "No way." I told her. "That's ridiculous! I definitely do NOT believe they are better than or superior to me." She calmly replied, "Go within and ask to be shown the truth. Go ahead. Ask again." I took a deep breath, quieted my mind, and put my hand over my heart. I asked my heart for the truth. I heard, *"Yes. It is true. There's a part of you that believes they are superior to you and that their needs are more important."*

I couldn't believe it! Did I really think they were superior to me? Then, I saw in my mind's eye...how my mother and grandmother believed the same thing: that the men in their lives were better than they were. I realized this limiting belief had been passed down to me through the generations. It was easy for me to see it in *them*, but I had no idea I was doing it, too. It was totally subconscious.

For the next few days, I did EFT (the Emotional Freedom Technique) on my subconscious belief that men (especially my husband and my boys) were superior. While doing EFT, I also realized that one of the reasons I felt this way was because my husband was the one who earned the money in our family. He was the "provider and protector." Therefore, even though I intellectually knew it wasn't true, my subconscious belief was that the source of my financial and physical security was my husband.

Once I accepted that I had limiting beliefs around my own self-worth, I worked to transform those beliefs. I would acknowledge my belief, choose to love and accept myself anyway, and then begin to create a new belief that would better serve me and my purpose:

- "Even though a part of me feels my husband and boys are more important than me, I deeply and completely love and accept myself."

- "Even though a part of me believes that male authority figures are superior and more powerful than me, I now choose to embody my highest truth: that I am as powerful, knowledgeable, and important as the men in my life."

- "Even though a part of me believes that my husband is the source of money and financial security in my life, I deeply and completely love and accept myself."

- "Even though I've made my husband the source of love, money and security in my life, I now know that the true source of love, money, and financial security in my life is God within me, and I choose to experience this truth in my life."

I find it interesting that in the last couple of weeks I've been working so deeply on the part of me that has felt lesser than others. I didn't realize I felt this way, but I am glad it was brought up to my attention in such undeniable ways so that I could finally shift those limiting beliefs.

12/16/15: I tried having another conversation with Matt yesterday. I told him that I realized that things were different between us, and I wanted to know if there was something specific that I had done to cause that. It took him a while to answer, and then he said, "No. Nothing specific. It's just who you are." Ouch. Who I *am*? How can I fix *that*? "But I like who I am," I thought. His answer hurt me so deeply.

I wasn't exactly sure how to reply to what he just said, so I told him I wanted us to be friends and support each other as we figured things out. As I talked, he felt like a brick wall. No emotion, no empathy. I felt like I was giving a monologue. He just kept clenching his jaw, taking deep breaths, and he'd only say, "Yes" or "Sure," and "We need to keep it 'business as usual' in front of the boys." When I asked him what "business as usual" meant and what that looked like, he kept repeating, "Business as usual. Business as usual."

I noticed he seemed to be getting more and more upset with me as I talked. Then he said, "You are oblivious. You are so naïve. You should have seen this coming." "Seen this coming?" I thought. I couldn't believe he actually said that. I could feel the anger bubbling up within me. Why didn't you *tell* me it was coming? I felt so many intense emotions as a result, but mostly I felt anger. I was so angry I wanted to hit him! And at the same time, I felt confused and sorry for myself. I had to get my thoughts straight in my head.

Later that evening, I wrote him a letter sharing how I felt. I wrote,

I am so disappointed at the way you've been treating me. I am done. I will not take this anymore. I am screaming inside, "Stop hurting me!" Stop taking me for granted. All I have done is love you and give you my best...and you can't see it. You judge it. You judge *me*. Your heart seems closed and you can't feel the love within it. Your closed heart is blinding you.

You say it is my fault that I didn't see it before. How could I see it if I've always chosen to see the positive in you and believe in you? I saw those challenging experiences as differences in opinion that we could eventually work out. I gave you space because I knew things were stressful at work and I assumed that's what you needed.

I always chose to put you first, before me. I gave you what I assumed you needed because I was afraid that asking you about it would create more disconnection or that you would reject me again. Well, it happened anyway! I need time to heal. I need gentleness in the weeks ahead.

I put the letter on his bed.

After I wrote the letter, I texted Loni, "I just had my conversation with Matt telling him my intentions to support each other as we tried to make things work. Jesus was right. His heart is so closed. I can't believe I didn't see it before. Ouch. It hurts. Doing my best to love myself right now."

She replied, "Jesus and your Team say, *As one door closes, another one opens. Center yourself. All the Love you need is within you. You are the Light. Project it brightly."*

Matt hasn't responded to the letter.

12/18/15: Matt still hasn't acknowledged my words. It's as if he never received them. I feel powerless. How could he do this to me? I, who have been the "perfect" wife and have dedicated my whole self to making sure he was happy and taken care of. The house is always in order, healthy meals have always been ready, the bills are always taken care of, the kids have been thriving at school. He's had his freedom, and I never complained: I am positive, playful, and have been a fun intimate partner.

He and the boys always have come first—their needs, their wants, their opinions, and thoughts. I always compliment him, express my appreciation in so many ways, give him space, make sure everything is always taken care of so that he doesn't have to worry about anything...because he works so hard to provide for our kids and me.

I am remembering that sometimes he has gone through phases when he would criticize me constantly. I would try to defend my point of view or how I did things, but it was rarely good enough for him. I also recognize that this did not happen all the time. There were also good times. There were times when we had fun, especially before last July, and I loved when he used to make me laugh.

I feel helpless. Why is this happening? How can I change it? *Can* I change it? I am losing hope.

12/19/15: The internet connection was not working today and the boys needed it working ASAP so they could finish their homework. I don't know much about internet connections, and Matt would not come home until late, so I figured I would call the cable company to help me. Unfortunately, they were not that helpful. When Matt got home, I told him what happened. He got upset with me because I didn't understand how to fix the router and my attempts to get technical help were not successful. He raised his voice at me. I knew this was an opportunity for me to stand up for myself and set boundaries, so I responded,

"Don't raise your voice at me. I can't count on you for anything. I had to figure this out on my own and I have to trust other people to help me. If they don't actually help me, that's not my fault."

It felt good to speak up…even though at the same time, I hate the tension and wish this whole thing were easier.

Funny how it had to get so bad for me in my relationship before I realized what a jerk he's been and how I was not empowered in my way of addressing him. No one should treat me like that. Even though I know I've co-created this, I need to be gentle with myself because I am still trying to figure out how to heal, love, and empower myself. I am still in the process of figuring out what that feels like, and what it looks like.

In the meantime, I keep doing EFT and telling myself, "I value myself. I am awesome. I am smart. I need to show him how to treat me better. I love myself..."

It's also been interesting to realize that with everyone else, it has been easy for me to be *me*! With others, I am self-confident and my bright, joyful, playful self. But with Matt, I am not like that. My light gets dimmer and I feel small. I notice that many times when he's around I can't think clearly; I feel needy and ignorant, and I doubt myself. I also tend to feel serious around him. Sometimes, I do try to be my joyful, playful self when he's around, but somehow it doesn't last long.

12/23/15: During this difficult journey, I've realized how important it is to take care of myself. These are some of the things I've been doing for the past two and a half months to take care of and love myself more:

- I start my days with a morning routine that helps me feel good and centers me.

- While I am still in bed, I start appreciating things, people, and anything I can think of. I usually start by saying, "I appreciate my comfortable bed," and then I go from there.

- I listen to guided meditations. These meditations help me to connect with my soul, open my heart, clear my energy, forgive, love myself, etc.

- I do gentle yoga. I love waking up gently and slowly. Stretching and moving my body helps bring blood flow back into my joints and muscles so that I can move my body more easily. Energetically, it also helps me feel balanced.

- I listen to Abraham Hicks's YouTube videos throughout my day…when I am driving, washing the dishes, folding laundry, walking, etc. I love Abraham's messages because they remind me of Who I Really Am, and how to manifest the life of my dreams in the easiest way.

- I do EFT (lots of it) whenever I feel emotional or feel I need to do inner work.

- I reach out to positive friends for support.

- I reach out to my Team for insights, clarity, and support.
- I go for walks as often as I can—ideally, daily.
- I go to Zumba on Saturday mornings.
- I am being extra gentle with myself: taking naps when I need to, simplifying my days, and not pushing myself to do too much.

12/26/15: Things have been even worse. I thought the Christmas spirit would make Matt lighter, but he is ignoring my presence totally, criticizing me, or making sarcastic comments. I am trying so hard to stay positive, but it hurts so much. This has been the saddest Christmas I've ever experienced. I feel totally abandoned.

***

Soon after I realized I had been taking on a victim mentality, I had the transformative experience I discussed in the intro. I meditated, prayed, and asked for guidance. How could I heal myself in the midst of so much hurt?

My Team said to me, *Love is the answer, and your brave journey will connect and strengthen those who are in their darkest moments, when they feel alone and abandoned.*

I was able to see how after this journey, which I began to call the "Master Course in Unconditional Self-Love," I would be better able to help others experience loving themselves, and to remind them in a very practical way that they are the source of the love they seek. I was grateful to be seeing the divine design of my journey and the gifts it offered.

I responded to my Team's words, "It is an honor for me to do this. This is *my* gift of Love. And I know that I could not do it in the best way possible if I had not gone through the experience myself. Yes, love is the answer, and the answer is within. Just like Jesus said, 'The kingdom of heaven is within.'"

1/13/16: I've been wanting to understand the higher reasons why this is all happening. I know that just like I can communicate with my Team, I can also communicate with Matt's Higher Self. I thought this would help me gain another higher perspective and help me see it from "his side." I opened my heart and connected with my soul. Then, I called in his Higher Self. I asked it for insights to help me understand. This is what Matt's Higher Self told me:

As you already know, I've had many lifetimes where I've either been very spiritually focused or have had a higher purpose in the role of warrior or soldier. In this lifetime, I wanted to live a normal life: one a regular man would live.

I need to know what pain feels like. In order to do that, I have to fall like all other angels in human form. I am not proud of this moment, but it's an experience I have to go through to gain higher consciousness. I am the one in the end who will truly suffer in this human form, but that's what my soul wants to experience.

You, Dumari, are getting the better end of this deal. You are going through the pain so that you'll end up with everything you want: love, joy, abundance, and fulfillment. I'm the one who will end up in pain, without love. But that is OK because ultimately, Love is who we are.

Know that I love you and I'll love you through this whole process.

I felt his deep love. My heart opened. I felt grateful for this message.

1/29/16: This morning, I am flying to Florida to take care of my mom, who is having major surgery today. I'm writing this on the plane on my way there. I'll stay in the hospital with her tonight and then in her apartment for another day or so. I want to make sure she can walk around on her own before I leave. I am grateful that she has friends and my brother who can keep an eye on her and help her out while she recuperates.

I've been reading Sonia Choquette's book *Walking Home*, which my Team suggested I read. Sonia's story is like mine in so many ways, especially her relationship with her husband, which ended in divorce. Walking the Camino helped her heal from that experience. In her book, she asked her guides what limiting beliefs she carried in her consciousness that had been keeping her from being her authentic Self. This inspired me to ask my Team the same question. This is what I heard them say.

You believe...

1. ...You are not good enough or valuable enough.

I said, "Not good enough? What do you mean?"

You believe you are not smart enough. You believe Matt is smarter than you, and you believe his opinions and needs are more valuable than yours.

2. ...That your boys and Matt's needs are more important than yours.

You give and give and give to them and don't look at or honor your own needs. You give yourself up for them.

3. ...That you may not make enough money to support yourself.

This makes you dependent on someone who you think is better than you in this area (making money).

4. ...That unconditional love means sacrificing yourself for those you love

and that in order to be a good mother and wife, you need to be unconditionally loving (a.k.a. sacrifice yourself). You got this belief from your mother.

5. ...That Love is only gentle, quiet, and nice.

It is not easy for you to see that Love can also be loud and strong, and sometimes, not so nice. For example, it's hard for you to see that standing up for yourself with your thoughts, words, and actions, including your body language, is the most loving thing you can do, not only for yourself, but for others as well.

6. ...That you ***need*** *to be loved and accepted by Matt in order to be happy.*

You fear being judged and rejected by Matt for being you, for showing who you really are: your empowered, wise, and bright self.

Wow! Thank you for these insights. I want to let go of these limiting beliefs once and for all. I know they don't serve me. I know they are not aligned with my higher truth. I do not want to be a victim of my limiting beliefs! I choose to empower myself fully and to embody my authentic self completely, no matter what.

I choose to shift these limiting beliefs now. Thank you God, my Higher Self, and my Team for helping me do so. I am taking each one of my limiting beliefs and choosing to shift them. This is what I claim, here and now, with the power of God (Divine Love) within me.

1. "I AM good enough. I am more than good enough; I am divinely perfect, whole, and complete. I AM smart, too! I am directly connected to the all-knowing source of wisdom and knowledge. I access it now, on demand. I remember to do this at all times. Whatever info I need, I access it at that moment, or it comes to me with perfect timing. This info can be about the spiritual world, as well as the physical world. I feel and know I am smart and wise. Yes, I AM!

2. "I choose to become fully aware of my needs, and to honor and value them. I will no longer put others' needs before mine. Nothing is more important than that I feel good because this is me loving God within me. I now realize this is the most important relationship in my life: my relationship with my Self. I choose to express my needs and welcome having them met. My needs are as important as my boys' and Matt's needs. It is MY responsibility to have my needs met first. I choose to express my needs with empowered love and confidence.

I promise to myself that I will do whatever I can to love and take care of all of me.

3. "I choose to fully know and experience God within me as the source of my abundance, including money, love, security, and everything I call good. I choose to become financially independent, fully trusting in the universe and my Higher Self to take care of me. And not only are my physical needs taken care of, but I also experience incredible wealth, so that I can fully experience the joy, freedom, comfort, and inner peace this brings. I can easily pay for my (and my boys') expenses and have lots of extra money to travel, pay for their college, go out for dinner, play, share with others, and enjoy life to the fullest.

   "I love all the inspired ideas and divinely orchestrated opportunities that come to me to expand my business. I love all the money that comes to me from my service to humanity and sharing my message. It is so rewarding, at so many levels, that my message and work empowering others from within brings me so much joy, fulfillment, and financial abundance.

"I free myself from any and all limitations regarding the source of money in my life. I finally set myself free and choose to experience my highest truth of infinite abundance.

4. "I choose to fully know and experience myself as being unconditionally loving. I choose to understand and embody the true meaning of unconditional love. Abraham says, *'Unconditional love is making your connection with your Source (your Inner Being) the most important thing so that no conditions will disconnect you from it.'*

   "I now understand that unconditional love has nothing to do with sacrificing myself! That's a very common misconception and one that is encouraged by many religions. I surely heard it many times in church when I was young. I am remembering Jesus' words in Paul Ferrini's book, *Love without Conditions*. There, he says, *'The first step to experience unconditional love is to love yourself* first.'

   "I can now see how Abraham is right and that loving unconditionally means making my connection with my

Inner being the most important thing. And that in order to do so, I just need to do whatever makes me feel good: choose the thoughts, words, and actions that feel the best to me, no matter what other people think, say, or do. I need to love myself first before I love anybody else. I have to fill my cup before I can give to others, otherwise I'll feel resentment. Unconditional love requires me to look within myself for love.

"I will no longer sacrifice myself in the name of love. I will honor and value my relationship with my Self, first and foremost. I will ask myself, 'Am I loving myself in this situation?' before I do anything. I will pay attention to how I feel as I am making choices that require giving. I will give to myself first, fill my cup with unconditional love, and then give unconditionally from that place of fullness. Then, I'll be able to give to others without conditions. I choose to be selfish in a loving way, so that everyone will benefit from my love being given freely. My joy is what I will share. I can only give what I have. I open myself to continue expanding my understanding and expression of unconditional love.

"I will no longer depend on others to be the source of love for me. I will no longer sacrifice myself in the name of love. I am choosing to F.L.Y.

F.L.Y = First. Love. Yourself.

5. "I choose to experience other expressions of love, besides 'gentle, soft, quiet, and nice.' I also choose to express love as powerful, loud, and bold. I will not limit love anymore. I choose to love myself and express the Divine Love that I am in whatever way is more authentic and aligned with Who I Really Am. I give my awesome, magnificent spirit a voice that is heard!

6. "I choose to release everything I am and have been attached to—my marriage and family, my reputation, my home, and comfort—in order to be fully in integrity with my authentic self. I choose to be ME, the awesome, bright, smart, wise, powerful and empowered, happy and joyful, clear, positive, sensual, spiritually aware, open-hearted, fabulous me! No matter what anyone, including Matt or any other authority figure, thinks, says, or does. I am no longer afraid of being judged or rejected because I am the source of love and acceptance

towards myself. I don't need anyone's approval to be me. I fully stand in my power. I choose to be me everywhere I am. Yay!"

These are my intentions and choices, my claims and promises to myself. I am excited to set myself free to be the real me in this lifetime. I do this with joy in my heart. My dear Team, thank you for your help and support in doing this. I specifically ask for awareness and reminders of my intentions as I move forward.

2/4/16: I am remembering the times in the last five months when I felt so sad—devastated, really. I feel a part of me died in the last five months...the part of me that looked up to Matt to feel loved and taken care of. Sometimes I've felt as if my world was crumbling down. As I write this, I hear my Team say, *It was crumbling down because it was not built on solid ground. The foundation was weak. It was external rather than internal.*

2/7/16: I received an email with a message from Mary Magdalene channeled by Tina Marie Daly. It is clear to me that it was divinely guided. I can hear her talking directly to me with these healing words...

I ask that you open your heart and hear my prayer for you. I hear your cries and feel the yearning of your heart. We indeed are in a time of great change; of letting go of that which no longer serves us, and stepping onto a path of real purpose and direction.

When you are releasing this energy it can feel as though you're losing a part of yourself, it can even feel like mourning a death because in reality, that's exactly what it is; a release of the "old you" dying to what no longer is in alignment with your highest truth and path, but because it's known and familiar to you, you hold on so tight afraid to let go. This can bring forth a period of confusion, loneliness and loss as you remain in fear of the unknown. But this is just the space in between what no longer is, and what hasn't completely already begun. It's an emptiness, but one necessary, to allow for a clean and open vessel for the new to enter. Trust my dear child and have faith in the unseen.

This change is actually what you have been praying for on a soul level. You just didn't expect it to show up in this fashion and last for so long. But this emptying out has been essential for the purification and evolution of your soul. Don't give up now just because it doesn't feel or seem the way you had hoped. That is just the earthly realm and human condition winning, and you are oh so much more that that! And you are more powerful beyond what you even realize!

You've come so far, and endured so much, and it's all to initiate you into a HIGHER level of your being. The blessings are there and will be revealed as you surrender, accept, and trust that it's all unfolding not only in according with your Divine Plan, but for the Greater Plan for All.

So please trust that although it has been a challenge, the reward is rich, beautiful and transformational. Soon, the heaviness will lift, the light will appear brighter, and you will not only see the direction you are heading, but feel a sense of renewal, rejuvenation, purpose, and an invigorated motivation to keep going!

2/9/16: I am getting the message that it is time for me to look at my fears about moving forward with a divorce. First, I received an email from Paul Ferrini reminding me that until I face my fears and learn the lessons they are offering me, I will continue to recreate the same difficult experiences I've been having.

I am also in the part in Sonia's book where she looks at her fears. It's now my turn. I want to be aware of them, learn from them, embrace them, see the highest truth, and ultimately, shift them into love.

My Team has told me for many years, *When Love Appears, Fear Disappears.* So I know that love is the answer that transmutes fear.

As I go within, these are some of the fears that are coming up as I consider getting a divorce:

- Fear of being financially independent. Can I make enough money doing what I love to cover all my expenses, support my boys, and be able to live a comfortable life? Or will I have to sacrifice once again by getting a job I don't enjoy?

- Fear of being by myself and having to be the only responsible adult in the home. Who will help me with the home maintenance and all the handyman things Matt used to do?

- Fear of having the boys suffer and miss their dad because he is not living with us anymore.

- Fear of having to work much harder and many more hours, which would leave me less time for myself and the things that fuel me.

- Fear of having to make all the decisions on my own without someone to bounce ideas off.

- Fear of not finding a beautiful home to live in. My home is so important to me. It is my sacred haven.

- Fear that separation and divorce happen too quickly, or before I am ready to do all these things on my own.

I am choosing to love these fears...and to love the parts of me that have these fears.

I am remembering reading in *A Course in Miracles* a few years ago that "fear stands for False Evidence Appearing Real" and that "Only Love is Real." These statements, combined with my Team saying, *When Love Appears, Fear Disappears,* are inspiring me to choose the highest truth of Love. And so, I AM choosing Love.

***

I had been feeling like a victim: first, I felt like the injured party in my marriage. When I recognized that I was replaying a narrative that women in my family had stepped in to time after time, I could finally see that I was also playing the victim to my own limiting beliefs. Matt wasn't to blame for my beliefs about my worth, my importance, and my intelligence. No one was, but it was my responsibility to face them head-on.

With guidance from my Team, I started to heal the limiting beliefs that kept me feeling small and powerless within my relationship and my life. I started realizing that I had some control, at least over my inner experience, and that I had the power to shift my perspective and beliefs.

***

Divine Insights from my Team

Victim. *You felt like a victim, with no control or power over what was going on in your relationship. But the truth is that you are never a victim. Ever! You set these circumstances into motion long before they happened. You chose them as your Higher Self before incarnating in this lifetime, and then, you chose them again with your thoughts and beliefs.*

Life is always conspiring in your favor. Everything unfolded in this way in order to give you the opportunity to create the experience of yourself that you've been yearning for. This was your creation, even if you were not consciously aware of it. It gave you a chance to become and to know, at the highest level, Who You Really Are.

Chapter 4: Overwhelmed

"People are like stained glass windows.
They sparkle and shine when the sun is out, but when the darkness sets in,
their true beauty is revealed only if there is a light within.
I wish I could show you when you are lonely or in darkness
the astonishing light of your own being."

—Elizabeth Kübler-Ross

By the beginning of the new year, I'd received insights from both my parents. I saw how I had taken on elements of my mom's insecurity, and I worked to love all of her and myself. With my dad's insights, I saw some of the ways in which I'd grown apart from myself and my innate sense of joy and playfulness. With these realizations, and with the support of my Team, I was starting to see a path forward.

I was able to get clearer on many things, especially how important it is for me to:

1. Reconnect with the joyful, bright Dumari
2. Truly love myself (and find out what that looks like for me)

I hoped that taking these actions would help with my relationship. After the tough holiday season, I was ready to turn the page—even if that meant turning away from my marriage. But I wanted to take the next step forward, whatever it would be, with Matt on the same page as me.

As my clarity that divorce might be the best choice grew, I wondered why this was happening to me now. Six months before, I had decided to grow my business, and my website had launched. Its name: Empower You From Within. How would divorce, and the things I was experiencing—Derailed, Isolated, Victim—help me with my work? With my message? I needed guidance about my marriage, and how its end related to my life's path.

I opened my heart to my Team's insights. However, once I was ready to face the end of my marriage, things got even harder. As I gained awareness of the truth of where Matt had been and what had happened to shift things between us, I felt angry. I felt alone once again. And most of all, I felt **Overwhelmed**.

***

1/7/16: During his visit, Dad helped me see how getting professional help from a marriage counselor would help Matt and I clarify what we both want. If we choose to stay together, we will be able to work on our relationship and communicate better with an expert's guidance. If we choose to separate, however, we will have the help we need to make the process harmonious, loving, and kind.

Either way, seeing a counselor is a good idea because our relationship needs to improve...for everyone's benefit, but especially for our boys. Ultimately, going to a marriage counselor will save the boys, Matt, and me a lot of pain.

My Team said that we should go to a male counselor, because Matt will respect him and listen to him more than to a woman. They also said that the counselor would be in Bedford, NH. I got the feeling that I would find him online, so I Googled marriage counseling in Bedford, NH and there he was! As soon as I landed on his webpage, I knew I'd found him.

I told Matt I found someone I wanted us to check out and he agreed to meet with him to see if it was a good fit.

1/15/16: Even though we haven't met with the marriage counselor yet, I am becoming more and more clear that the highest outcome involves getting a divorce. That's the only way I can finally get what I truly desire. I know Matt can't give me what I want in a relationship. It's time for me to be free from being disempowered and be free to be me!

It has taken me a few days to integrate my decision into every cell of my body. The more time that passes, the surer I am that this is the highest choice. When I think, "I am getting a divorce," I feel free. I feel empowered. I feel scared and sometimes overwhelmed. I feel trusting. I feel happy. I feel sure and certain of my decision.

Tonight, I looked at him with my newly found certainty. When I felt his energy, which felt harsh and distant, I thought, "Wow. This really IS the best thing I can do for myself! OK Team, here we go! I am jumping off the cliff, spreading my beautiful wings, opening my heart, and shining my light. Thank you in advance for catching me and helping me create a fabulous path for me to land softly on and to follow towards my greatest destiny!" I affirmed my trust in the universe that I would be taken care of and everything would be all right.

1/16/16: This morning I did yoga. I love the routine I've created for myself in the mornings: appreciating, meditating, and gentle yoga. It centers me. It clears my head and emotions. I feel grounded and more flexible. It's as if my energy can flow more easily through my body and mind.

Today is Saturday, so I also went to Zumba. Gosh, I love Zumba. It is so much fun! I love to dance and move my body to Latin music. So sensual. So happy. It's like I am at a joyful party. Doing it also makes me feel strong. Liz's class is very physical. I feel my heart pumping and my body breathing hard. I sweat. It's such a great workout.

I also went for a walk this afternoon. My intention for my walk was to get myself feeling really good and to increase my vibration. I wanted to get into "my vortex," what Abraham calls my good-feeling vibrational place where everything I want is already a reality. Oh my…did I get there. I felt awesome. I appreciated so many things…my body, myself, my experiences with Matt for the growth and empowerment resulting from all this, nature, the sun, the sky, my friends and loved ones, my boys, my Team, my future clients...

During my walk, I started anticipating my bright future: my independence, my amazing lover, my clients, my work, my new home, my abundance, having so much fun with myself and those I love, playing, etc.

My dad called and we talked for a while. It is always so wonderful to talk to my dad.

I loved today. I treated myself to all these things that make me feel so good. Yep, I sure loved myself today.

1/18/16: I haven't told Matt about my decision yet, but I wonder if he can feel it. I wonder if he can feel my emotional detachment from him. Last night he was so nice to me. He was even playful, calling me "hottie" and "baby." I have to confess that my heart melted and I was wondering if I had made the right choice.

My Team had warned me about this last week. They said that he would show signs of being affectionate and attracted to me. They asked me what I would do if he did. They wanted me to be prepared for when it happened. And here it was!

I asked for clarity as I fell asleep last night. Clarity came at 3 a.m.! I was woken up at that time and heard my guys say,

You made the right choice. Matt has been and can be very cruel. You want someone whose heart is so open that that behavior wouldn't even cross their mind. If he does in fact change through the process of marriage counseling, he'll have to prove it to you. It will not serve you to continue giving him the benefit of the doubt without him doing much to deserve it. Your relationship will get better through this process of marriage counseling, but ultimately, you will not experience everything your heart really desires within this relationship.

1/20/16: I was listening to Sonia Choquette's interview about *Walking Home*. She was talking about her divorce, the death of her dad and brother, and how walking the Camino helped her heal from these traumatic events. In the interview, she said that she realized she stuffed down and denied her negative feelings towards the people that hurt her because as a spiritual person, she understood why her loved ones did what they did to her. I wonder if I am doing or have been doing the same thing.

I asked my Team for any insights they could share with me on this. I heard,

Throughout your relationship and marriage, you did deny your feelings and your pain. You usually tried to see things from his perspective first, and you devalued what you thought and felt. But in all fairness, that' s not necessarily a bad thing. It helped you cope.

Looking at things from a higher perspective helped you gain peace and be happy regardless of the conditions you were experiencing. With the limiting beliefs you held about yourself, not feeling the pain was a survival mechanism. You were not ready to face that pain or the limiting beliefs then.

That has changed in the last year. With the completion of your website last Spring, along with the spiritual growth you've gone through in the process, you are now ready to face your biggest

fears and limiting beliefs. You were not ready to empower yourself fully from within until now!

Once you go through this process yourself, you will be able to fulfill your highest work in service of others. You knew there was something missing within you before you could fully step into doing your work at the highest level. This was it. This was the missing piece. You were still depending on someone else. You did not value or honor yourself fully. You had not been in a position where you needed to rely on your own source to survive.

Matt is doing you a huge favor. He's giving you a beautiful gift! He is "abandoning" you. He will no longer fully love you or support you, so you have to look for the source of love and support within yourself.

When you experience this, only then, will you be "qualified" to teach and show others that they can do it, too. You need to be authentic, an embodied example of what you came here to teach and demonstrate: Empowering Yourself From Within.

You needed to know that God (Love) within you is the source of everything you need, and you needed to know how to experience this in practical ways in your daily life. You also needed to love yourself more. Get to experience unconditional love, love without conditions— love yourself so much that you choose to stay connected to the source of love within you no matter what the conditions around you are.

Even though it appears that Matt is the "bad" guy here, his beautiful soul, who is your eternal friend, agreed to do this for you. He has forgotten this. So regardless of what appears to be the cause of his negative behavior towards you, this is all part of what you both agreed to go through before you incarnated in your human bodies. Love him for this...because his spirit loves you eternally. Now, this does not mean to give yourself up to love him. Honor and value yourself, and be compassionate towards him at the same time. Find the fine balance.

This is not all about you, either. Matt's soul also has an agenda. He has some lessons and experiences to go through. Plus, he has free will. It's true that he's closed his heart and that his Higher Self is having a hard time reaching him, but that's ok. It will all work out. You never get it done and you never get it wrong.

...And back to denying your feelings...this past year you've been facing your biggest fears and limiting beliefs. You are no longer denying anything.

The Tough Mudder helped you create the foundation for this shift. It prepared you. Then, Matt stepped in with full force to fulfill his role to help set you completely free from all co-dependency you had on anything outside of yourself.

1/22/16: I found this from Neale Donald Walsch in my inbox today. I love how my Team continues sending me encouraging messages!

> On this day of your life,
> Dear Friend, I believe God wants you to know...
>
> ...that there will come a time when you believe everything is finished. That will be the beginning.
>
> Louis L'Amour said that, and he was right. We must let go. All of it. It will look as if your life is over, and that everything you have worked for has collapsed. Actually, its construction will have just begun.
> It is so trite, I know, but I must say it anyway. I have to say it.
> 'For every door that closes, there is another that opens.'

This is the door you have been *looking* for...

But you could not hope to find it while you were locked behind the first one.

1/23/16: Last night, I just had turned off the lights and was falling asleep when I heard my Team say, *Google emotional abuse.* At first I thought, "Really? Now? I was just looking forward to falling asleep!" But I felt a strong urge to do it at that time and I know it serves me to follow my inner guidance. When I hear my Team say something that clearly, I do it. At least I try to. What I found surprised me and at the same time gave me a sense of relief.

The first result was a blog post, "30 Signs of Emotional Abuse in a Relationship." I clicked on it and went through each sign. I ended up checking "Yes" to 19 out of the 30 signs. Oh my! What I was experiencing had a name...."Emotional Abuse!" And neither of us was aware of it.

I found it interesting that this morning when I told my mom how many signs I found, her response was, "Oh, it's not that many. At least it's not ALL of them." I couldn't believe what I just heard. No wonder it was so hard for me to identify what was happening. A part of me thought it was normal because that's what had been passed down to me through the generations.

Another VERY interesting thing that happened to me today is that my Team said to me,

Now that you have clarity about your decision to get a divorce and the purpose of this experience for each of you, it's important that you focus on Matt's positive aspects. This will help you get to a place of acceptance, appreciation, understanding, and ultimately, forgiveness.

If you want to improve your relationship, set yourself completely free, and create the highest outcome, it is critical that you do this. Plus, it will help you be in vibrational alignment with the amazing relationship waiting for you in your vortex. So appreciate him! Be on the lookout for his positive aspects.

I wrote 5 pages of positive qualities and aspects that I could think of in Matt. My Team was right. This was very helpful! I felt good doing this.

1/24/16: My prayer today:

"Dear God, universe, and my support system out there,

"Thank you for your insights, guidance, and loving encouragement. Thank you for helping me break free from everything that has bound me, kept me small, and dimmed my bright light. I realize that my unhappiness is a sign from my spirit to let me know I am not totally aligned with my highest truth.

"I want to be free from these limiting beliefs and patterns. I want to be happy! I choose to experience and express the highest truth of my being. Help me access my inner strength to let go of all that I have created up until now, on every level, which no longer serves me. Help me release everything that no longer reflects the highest path for me and for those who I love and am here to serve.

"Help me face and shift my fears. Help me experience the courage and empowerment I need in order to make these changes with ease, joy, and confidence. Thank you for giving me the clarity to know what the next highest steps are for me. I want to fulfill my heart's desires in every area of my life and I claim these as mine now. I am ready and looking forward to manifesting my greatest, most joyful, and most fulfilling life with passion. I choose to do this with Divine Love as my guide. For this and so much more, I am so grateful!"

***

Some of the questions I was asking at this time weren't new. A year before, in early 2015, I had asked my Team for deeper insights about my life's work. In January of that year, I had a written conversation with my soul. It gave me a deeper understanding about why all this is happening.

I said: "I want to know more about my life's work." I asked my soul for more clarity about it. This is what I heard:

The world needs you now. The real you. The bold you. The bright light you. The empowered and powerful you. You are an answer to a prayer. Affirm that fear and limitation no longer have power over you. Embody your destiny of greatness, of purpose and infinite power. You are brilliant, gorgeous, and a magnificent being of light, abundance, beauty, and infinite potential. You are love and wisdom beyond imagination. This is the truth of your being.

I asked my soul, "If I could live my life at its highest level—If I could be, do and have, create and contribute fully—what would that look like?"

My soul responded,

You would be happy beyond belief. You would be touching thousands of lives every day.... helping people remember their highest truth: that they are God, perfect, whole, and magnificent. You'd be sharing that there's nothing to fear because they are the power of Love itself. That they have the power to be, do, and have their heart's desires with EASE. That they are never alone, but always loved and supported by unconditionally loving and incredibly wise non-physical beings whose greatest joy is to support them in experiencing joy and fulfillment.

I asked, "If I could have all my needs (physical, emotional, spiritual) met with ease, what would I do?"

My soul said,

You would have fun in everything you do. Joy would radiate from your pores all the time (even as you experience the contrast)! You would never doubt yourself or life. You would embody the Christ within you and you would KNOW it. And your greatest joy would be to awaken others to THEIR Christ within.

You would be a super BRIGHT light unto the darkness. You would be writing for many to read, speaking for many to hear, and presenting for many to see. And all this you will do and more! You are ready. You have set the highest vision for yourself into motion. Get ready for the ride of your lifetimes!

We love you. We adore you. We guide and support you all the way…all the time. Believe in yourself. We DO!

We are your soul and awesome Team. ☺

Then, I added, "If I were living the life of my dreams, these would also be true…

- My finances would be totally abundant and flowing. I would have so much money that I could easily take care of all my needs and wants to enjoy this life fully. I would have enough money to take care of my children and have plenty more to share with others.

- My body would be my ideal weight and shape.

- ALL my relationships would be joyful, supportive, positive, easy, and fun.

- I would have balance of time to enjoy myself, my family and friends, and my work with ease."

I asked my soul, "Is there anything else I can add that would make it even better?" I heard,

Totally trust yourself, and that God speaks through you and as you clearly and with ease. Just as God spoke through Jesus (and other messengers in today's world), you have the same ability and talent within you. You were born to do this. Trust that the highest wisdom and knowing can flow through you with the same clarity and ease as other spiritual masters have possessed.

This is the next step for you. You will get to experience this. Practice it as you create more opportunities to do this through your writing, videos, talks, trainings, and sessions.

I asked, "Am I leaving anyone out from this vision? Is there someone I want to bring with me? A family member, a partner, a group? Who do I want to do this with?"

Of course you wish to bring Matt with you. You've always wanted to do so. And understand that part of the agreement you made together before coming to this lifetime is that he would neither see nor understand your work and mission. Part of his purpose is to live a mainstream, normal life. This will offer him the lessons his soul wishes to experience.

One thing that he may be able to give you is support and respect for what you do, even when he doesn't understand it. This may satisfy your desire to bring him along. Honor and respect his journey. Through your example, he'll grow. His heart will open more to love. He'll become aware of how his judgments and closed heart limit him. Eventually, he may even become aware of his inner child, who is hurting and doesn't feel safe or good enough in this world.

You do not need to force his spiritual growth. That is not your responsibility. He is not your client and doesn't want to be! The best thing you can do for him is to see his highest potential. See him happy and living with an open heart.

One of the gifts he is offering you with his judgment of your work is for you to believe in yourself, even when those close to you don't.

I asked, "Who am I doing this for?"

I answered, *I am doing this for all who are searching for a higher truth…a more loving, joyful, and easy way of life. Those searching for connection with their Source (God), and their own spirit…a connection with Divine Love and a higher Truth. Those who want to awaken to Who They Really Are…and to experience more peace, ease, and fun in their lives.*

I am also doing this for me…for my own spiritual growth. I want to teach what I most want to experience myself! I experience it and share it. Then, as I share it, I master it in an even deeper way.

Reflecting on these insights, I saw that my path had taken me exactly where my Team said it would. I hadn't foreseen divorce, but I had known that my marriage often challenged me to believe in myself and love myself. Now that things between Matt and I had shifted, I was ready to ask for further insights. This is what I heard a year later in 2016:

You are going through this major challenge in your life so that you can fulfill your soul's purpose, both for yourself, as well as in service to others. How can you teach and model this to others if you haven't fully experienced it yourself? If you haven't felt and experienced the fears, the challenges, the doubt, and the sadness they have? Then, with the tools and knowing you are gaining, you will bring yourself out of the darkness and into the light. You will lead by example. Then, and only then, will they be able to trust you because you've been there and you've mastered what they wish to master themselves.

It is highly unlikely that Matt will satisfy your desire to have a supportive partner with you in this area. You need to make the choice as to whether this is something you are willing to live without or not. We understand that there are other things you desire in your relationship that he is not able to provide. You can still fulfill these desires with someone else. This is your choice...and he (Matt's Higher Self) knows this. He needs to go through his own lessons.

***

2/10/16: Today, I had a call with Vicki, my Mastermind colleague, who is also an intuitive. During our call, I asked for some direction as to what I should focus on in my work after concluding my "Parenting Through Your Heart" group coaching program. I mentioned that I planned to work on updating my H.E.A.R.T.S. Way to Divine Guidance program that I've been wanting to complete for some time. She said, "I get a no for that. I get that in May you'll be starting to pack and getting ready to move."

"Oh no! So soon?" I said, while feeling fear bubbling right up—big time. This is too quick for me! I had to go for a walk. I needed to shift the energy of fear I was feeling. I needed to get into "my vortex." I am glad I did.

I had a beautiful walk. It was snowing out: it was bitter cold and windy, but I went all the way to my favorite spot, the apple orchard up the hill from my house. On my way back, my Team gave me a message through nature. I was already in my vortex, feeling so much appreciation for myself, for Matt, for my Team, and for my life.

On my way back, I noticed there were many birds singing around me, and even though I couldn't see them, I could *hear* them. Their song was loud...and so beautiful. I heard myself say in my mind,

"That's my song of Joy! The birds singing represent me singing the song of joy within my heart. Even when the conditions around me show no evidence of the source of joy, I can still hear my beautiful song."

Then, I noticed how warm I felt inside, even though it was frigid cold, snowing, and gray outside. I felt cozy and comfortable inside of myself. Again, even if the outside conditions showed one thing, I was having a different experience within me. As I noticed this, I heard my Team say,

This is how it will be in the months ahead. Even though going through a divorce may seem cold and gloomy, with no conditions to encourage happiness, your inner experience will be different. You will be comfortable and happy inside.

"Thank you, guys, for this beautiful and comforting message!" I told them with heartfelt appreciation.

***

As I grew more accustomed to the idea of divorce, I was feeling better—happy, even. Finally, I was ready to move on. But first I had to understand what I was moving on from.

Matt had been coming home late for seven months, and he would say he was just out with the guys. Our sexual connection was gone, and so was our romantic connection. He'd been spending more money than usual. I wanted to stop feeling hurt, and to get to a place of understanding so that I could move towards my highest purpose.

I talked to Suzie, a colleague who is very much connected to her Team. I asked her if she could ask her Team for any insights about what had been happening in my marriage.

She said, "I am hearing that there is a part of you that is afraid of finding out the truth."

"What truth?" I asked.

She said, “They say that I can’t tell you anything more. That it is important that you do find out the truth, but you have to do it yourself.”

I hung up surprised at what I heard.

I had a serious conversation with my Team and told them I was ready to know. I was ready to peel back the remaining layers of fear. I had to know the truth. I meditated. I tapped on my fears. I asked to be shown the truth.

And soon, I started seeing in my mind’s eye what had been going on with Matt and where he’d been these past months. As the scenes flashed through my mind, I felt as if my heart was being ripped apart. The pain was almost unbearable. How could he do this to me? I trusted him. I believed in him. I was there for him.

I felt totally betrayed. Abandoned. And what felt worst was the lying, the constant hiding all these months. I felt he took advantage of me, of my innocence, of my trust. I felt he took a part of my soul. “Oh God, please help me,” I cried for help to get me through this as the warm tears flowed down my face. I felt so weak I could barely walk.

***

3/7/16: I just realized what has truly been going on with Matt all these months. Everything is making sense now. The shift in his energy and behavior, the change between us. Even though it is obvious to me now, I am still shaken. This is totally overwhelming. And still, I have to muster the strength to keep going and be there for my boys.

I am at Conway ice arena waiting for John to be done with his ice hockey practice. I am sitting by myself in the lobby writing in my journal…I am having a wicked intense contrast attack! I am ANGRY! I am PISSED! How come I didn't see it before? How could he do this? I am screaming inside. I feel all this pent-up emotion—like a volcano that wants to erupt.

I am also angry with Matt's best friend. All those late nights together—he'd known what was happening, and even encouraged it. I've never liked him. My gut told me I couldn't trust him, even when he was so "nice" towards me. I felt he was faking. This is helping me get more clear on how my gut talks to me and how to discern when it is telling me something.

Wait...I am hearing a familiar voice. I can't believe this...I just looked to my left and there he is, Matt's best buddy. How interesting is that? I had no idea he would be here. His son is probably on the ice, too. OK, I have a choice. Like my Team has told me before, *"Will you choose Love or fear?"*

I am choosing Love. Even when it's *really* hard, I choose to be Love. What will that look like now? We'll see. Jesus, help me be Love, like you are Love. I choose to see through the eyes of Source; through the eyes of Love. A feeling of peace and understanding is filling me inside. A sense of compassion. Yes, I am getting it. I am understanding their humanness. I accept it and embrace it with Love. And I choose to love *my* humanness, too. I choose to love my anger. I choose to love all of me through this emotionally hard time.

Oh shoot. He just saw me. And off course, he is being loud and obnoxious about it. He's coming over...

All right, he just left. The first thing he told me was, "Oh, look who's here? I was checking you out before I realized it was you! And why didn't you say hello? Are you being a snob?"

Did I hear that right? Did he just say he was checking me out...in front of all the hockey parents at the rink? And then he called me a snob? I feel insulted and disrespected. But hey, why should I expect anything else from this guy?

3/11/16: After the incident with Matt's friend, I texted Matt right away to let him know what had happened. No response. I waited two more days. Nothing. Not even when he saw me at home that night and the next couple of nights afterwards. Wow. This hurts.

While in the shower today, I couldn't help but feel so alone, so abandoned, so vulnerable. I sobbed. The hot water was running down my face and my body as I cried. The intense emotions I felt were so painful. My heart was aching. I tapped, right there in the shower. I needed some relief. As I tapped, I realized that I was expecting Matt to protect me, defend me, and take care of me. Another realization of something I felt I *needed* from him.

I remembered that I am the source of everything I perceive I need, including being protected, defended, and taken care of. So I affirmed, "I AM the source of protecting me, defending me, and taking care of me."

Then, I heard my Team say,

Yes, you are the source of all these, but you don't always have to be the channel of it. It is OK to have someone else, your partner in this case, express their love in the form of protecting, defending, and taking care of you.

Oh, I liked hearing that. Deep within me, I want to experience that in a relationship.

Tonight, I finally had to say something about it to him. I asked Matt what he thought about his friend's comments to me. He said, "He is an idiot. I am not going to defend him. I talked to him the next day and told him it was not appreciated. But you know that's how he is. Don't pay attention to him."

Hmm, his answer doesn't make me feel that much better. Why didn't he tell me he did that? I feel he really doesn't care about how I feel. It makes me sad, but I am understanding more and more the importance of not allowing my feelings to depend on his actions. I am working on this.

3/12/16: Finding out the truth is really hitting me hard. On one end, I feel relieved that I finally know the cause of Matt's change in behavior and that everything makes sense now. On the other hand, I am wondering why didn't I see this sooner. Why didn't my intuition tell me many months earlier? I am starting to lose faith in my inner guidance. Everything is so obvious now, but I couldn't see it then. Will I be able to trust my intuition moving forward?

A sense of peace is coming over me. I can feel my Team telling me,

Be gentle with yourself. Forgive yourself for not seeing clearly earlier. You CAN trust your intuition moving forward. You have learned so much from this experience. There were many reasons why you didn't see clearly before. There were expectations and fears in the way, but you've grown so much—you will not be blindsided again. It's important that you keep your heart open and continue trusting your inner guidance.

3/13/16: I have a throbbing headache. I am feeling overwhelmed with emotions. I am having a really hard time integrating the truth I just faced. I feel so hurt!

I am asking my Team to help me let go of these painful thoughts and help me stay in my heart. Out of the blue, I am hearing the Beatle's song "Let It Be" in my mind...I can feel Mother Mary's energy comforting me as I hear the song play in my head. I start crying...as I let it be.

3/16/16: Oh my, what a week and a half it's been for me. I'd say this has been one of the most intense and overwhelming weeks of this whole journey. I feel like the darkest times of my journey have been leading to this past week. They were leading me to the final piece, the ultimate climax. I finally found out the truth! I finally can set myself free! I AM free! No more guessing why he's been treating me this way for the last seven months. No more wondering. The truth shall set me free...and it has!

I find it amusing how my body is reacting to this. Tuesday night around 3 a.m., I got a really intense pain in my left ear. I

Googled what to do and took some Advil. The pain went away, but my ear was filled with fluid.

When I went to the doctor to have it checked out, they did a hearing test. I had almost no hearing in that ear. I know that our bodies serve as messengers to us, so I asked my body and my Team what the message was. I heard, *The truth is too hard to hear.*

Yep. It made sense, so I started to do the inner work right away. I worked on releasing any and all fears related to this.

My Team said,

Dumari, what do you want moving forward? You already know the truth, so what do you want next? The most important thing you can do is for you to get clear about what you want. What is the highest relationship you want to have with him in order to parent your boys in the most empowering and peaceful way? What does it look like and feel like moving forward?

You have gone as deep as you can go within this relationship. You've hit rock bottom. Now, come from your heart. Get specific about how you want the relationship to look and feel in the weeks and months to come, and even after you are divorced. How do you want to communicate? How do you want to relate? Be specific.

You need to get as clear about the details as possible. Focus on how you will feel. This will help you make this a reality.

They also added,

Matt has shifted his perspective about you for some time now. In his eyes, you are no longer his wife. He sees you as a business partner. You are there to take care of the kids, the house, and things that need to get done. And he is paying you for your services by taking care of you financially. He's never told you, but that's the way it is.

Thank you guys for putting it so bluntly. It actually helps.

You know, sometimes it all gets to be too much. Sometimes I feel paralyzed. I can't think clearly. Sometimes, I can't think period. It's like my mind goes blank.

Some days I just have no energy, no motivation. Sometimes, I just have so much to do, and I don't know if I can do it all. And yet at times, my emotions are so intense...the feelings of anger, sadness, abandonment, disappointment, and feeling betrayed. How can I keep going? It all feels too overwhelming.

My inner guidance is telling me that in order to shift these feelings of being overwhelmed by all these thoughts (of what has happened, is happening and will happen), *AND* the intense emotions I feel, I need to:

- Get clear on what I really want
- Get into my vortex as often as I can...by doing whatever I can to feel better
- Continue loving myself in very practical ways every day:
    - With my morning centering routine
    - Do things I love and/or that make me feel good
    - Simplify my days
    - Rest when my body tells me to
    - Be gentle with myself
    - Address the emotions that come up in whatever way I get guided to
    - Reach out to my positive friends for support
    - Reach out to my Team and pay attention to their signs

- Follow my inner guidance telling me how to empower myself through this process, and/or whatever it is I need at the time

I LOVE you, guys! I don't know what I would do without you. I am so grateful to have you in my life. Thank you.

***

Divine Insights from my Team

Overwhelmed*. The intense emotions you felt, as well as feeling that it was all too much for you to handle, made you feel overwhelmed. Feeling overwhelmed paralyzes you. You feel incapable of moving forward.*

Even though this is a natural effect resulting from what you experienced during this time, you can shift this feeling of overwhelm so that you feel empowered to move forward. It is a matter of perspective. The way you look at things will determine how you feel about them. Once you start shifting your perspective, it is easier for you to think clearly and to start taking action. Even taking small steps is enough. It creates the momentum that gets you closer to your desired destination.

The perspective that is most important for you to shift is that it is all too much for you. This applies to both your emotions and things you feel you have to do.

The truth is that you can bring yourself to a state of calm, clarity, and ease, regardless of what is going on in your life. It's important to love and accept yourself through it. You can then ask your soul and Team for a higher perspective on the situation, and for ways you can focus on what is really important and will make the greatest positive impact in your life.

Remember that whatever is going on in your life is giving you an opportunity for something greater to emerge through you and as you. You have the power to shift overwhelm into calm; confusion into clarity; and stress into ease.

Chapter 5: Refocused

"In the end, she became more than what she expected.
She became the journey, and like all journeys,
she did not end, she just simply changed directions and kept going."

—R.M. Drake

Because I felt overwhelmed by so many of the events after the new year, I knew I needed to **Refocus** on myself. I couldn't control Matt, but I could control my own experience. And with the insights from my Team, I knew that I needed to focus my attention and energy on something other than my feelings of Derailment, Isolation, and Overwhelm.

Many days brought new challenges. Matt and I started marriage counseling, and as you know, I learned the truth about his behavior in March. In the middle of that pain, it was important to start focusing on loving myself—what that looked like and felt like. This was the first step in gaining clarity on the direction I wanted my life to go in.

By Valentine's day, I was ready to begin a journey towards loving myself more. When I discovered a "40 Day Affair With Yourself" program, I knew it was a perfect fit. In those 40 days, I started falling in love with myself and getting clear on what I wanted my life to look like in the months and years ahead.

During this phase is when things started shifting and becoming brighter. Knowing that I was getting a divorce, I focused on my ideal life and what I really wanted; I tried to feel and see myself living that life, which shifted my energy. I started smiling again. My soul was joyful. I was feeling stronger. Finally, the path ahead was clear—and I was enjoying myself as I walked along it.

***

2/12/16: Today, I went out to lunch with my girlfriend Loni. We had a good time, and it was also very productive. While at the restaurant, my Team said to me,

It's now time for you to start getting clear about what you want. It's important to have clarity about what you want your life to look like: starting now, through the separation, and after the divorce. Once you know what you want, start envisioning it and feeling how good it will feel.

They gave me some suggestions to help me get started. First, they suggested I get a piece of paper and a pen. "Got it!" I said.

Then, they asked, *What do you want the theme of your life to be?* I thought for a moment, "Hmmm…Happiness?" I said.

They had another suggestion, *How about Endless Joy?*

"Perfect!" I said.

They suggested I write my new theme as the title on the top of the piece of paper and make four lists underneath it: House, Wealth, Life, and Work.

I created an outline, along with some divinely inspired suggestions from them.

- House:

- *This is the first thing to focus on because you want to move during the summer before your boys start school in September,* they said.

- **Size.** *How big do you need your new place to be? How many bedrooms? How about the kitchen and living space?*

- **Location.** *Where do you want to be? Which town? Close to the boys' school? What type of area do you want to live in? How about the neighborhood? Do you want to be able to go for walks in a beautiful and convenient setting? Do you want to feel safe?*

- **Characteristics (must haves and nice to haves).** *Do you want a garage? How about windows to let in natural light? What would you like your office space to feel like? What would you like the bedrooms to feel like? How about storage space? Do you want an older home or a newer one? How about renting or buying, and how much would you like to pay monthly?*

- Wealth:

- **Finances.** *How much do you need every month? How much would you like to have every month? Create a detailed budget!*

- **Savings.** *How much would you like to have in Savings? How much would you like to have saved for emergencies, or for traveling to see your mom? How about debt?*

- **Financial freedom!** *What does that look like? How does that feel? Get specific.*

- **Alimony & Child Support.** *You will focus on this in more detail once the divorce proceedings are under way.*

- My Life:
    - **Health & body.** *What do you want your body to feel like? What would you like your body to look like?*

    - **Time management** (balance between "me" time, work, friends, family, play, etc.). *What do* *you want your days to look like? Your weeks? Your months? Your life in general? Take into consideration what you want to do with your time.*

- **Fun & Play.** *You tend to work too much. Even personal things can become 'projects' to work on. We suggest you take time to play more. How would you like to enjoy yourself, play, and have more fun?*

- **Loved-ones, friends and connection with others.** *Envision your relationships and how you want them to be. What do you want your relationship with your children to be like? With your parents, your friends, others around you? How do you want to be supported?*

- **Boundaries.** *One area we'd like you to focus on is redefining your boundaries with your boys. Reteach them how to value and respect you so you don't repeat the cycle. See yourself in your new role: an empowered woman and mother (i.e. "the boss," not "the maid.")*

- Work:
    - *You already have a general idea of what you want to do in this area, but you will focus on it in more detail once you are in your new space.*

As soon as I got home, I got to work. I started creating my ideal home and my ideal life in my mind. I wrote it down. I envisioned the details, and most importantly, I focused on how it would make me *feel.* It felt wonderful!

After I was done with my exercise, I heard my Team say,

Know that everything that you want is already done. Even if you can't see it in your physical reality yet, it is happening in a vibrational reality. This is what Abraham-Hicks calls "the vortex." It's as if your favorite song (a.k.a. your ideal life) is playing on a radio station somewhere out there. It is already playing. And in order for you to hear it, all you have to do is tune your radio dial to match that radio station. When you start singing your song in your head, then out loud with gusto, and then dance to it while it's playing in your head—that's how you get to manifest and hear your favorite song in your reality. The more fun you have doing this, the faster you'll hear your song playing in your life!

2/14/16: Happy St. Valentine's Day, Dumari!

This is so cool...Last week, I decided that I would have a love affair with myself! I thought it would be fun. "First, I will start with having a love affair...with me," I said to myself. "Then, I will get engaged...to me. And later, I will end up marrying...*me*! Perfect." LOL!

In all seriousness, I feel it is important that I do this...I need to truly fall in love with myself first, before I can have my ideal relationship with someone else.

I love how the universe works. This morning, I received an email in my inbox that caught my eye. From the moment I saw the title, I knew it was divinely guided. The title said, "Have an affair with yourself." Is this real? I was laughing! Oh my...It couldn't have been more perfect! It was an invitation to join Karen Paolino's online program, *"40 Day Affair with Your Self, A Journey of Self Love and Owning Your Magnificence."* Need I say more? I signed up right away!

2/19/16: I went for a walk with Loni today. During our walk, I received some helpful and interesting insights from my Team. I wanted to understand more deeply why this was happening in my relationship. Early last summer, things seemed to be going so well and I was so happy. Then, by the end of the summer, things became painful—the feeling of derailment set in.

My Team said there were three main reasons for this:

1. **Soul Agreement:** Matt and I agreed to go through this experience for the benefit of our souls' agendas. They said we've already talked about that.

2. **Vibrational Mismatch:** I was feeling so good this past summer creating my ideal life in my mind, going into "my vortex," and feeling so happy, that my vibration went high. Matt couldn't match it. Our vibrations became too different. That's when things started crumbling.

3. **Lack of Clarity on my Part:** Before, I wasn't totally clear about what I wanted in a relationship. This lack of clarity prevented me from seeing that Matt had not provided nor allowed for what my soul really wanted.

Plus, a part of me was emotionally attached to Matt, so I was willing to sacrifice myself in order to be with him. It was very hard for me to let go of him. Once I got clear about what I wanted and detached myself emotionally from having him meet that, the "pain and suffering" went away.

Getting clear on the relationship I desired was a good beginning, and then, I needed to detach myself emotionally from him...to move into unconditional love, starting with loving myself no matter what.

2/20/16: I found this email from Neale Donald Walsch in my inbox. It reminded me of the purpose of life and its challenges. Thank you for the reminder, guys!

> On this day of your life,
> Dear Friend, I believe God wants you to know...
>
> ...that challenges are what you came for. And you are
> never, *ever*, given a challenge you cannot overcome.

> The purpose of life is to give you a chance to be the grandest version of the greatest vision ever you held about Who You Are. When challenges arrive, then, move straight to clarity: *This is what you came for.*
>
> Now rise to this occasion, and know that you have every resource with which to create the right and perfect outcome.

2/21/16: I was talking to my friend Swati last week about what was happening with me and my divorce these days. She said that she keeps seeing me writing a book about my divorce journey. She said that she felt it would help many women see that divorce could be something positive in their lives and that I could show them how it could even be fun. I had a hard time envisioning myself writing a book about my relationship challenges. I had too many questions of what would be in that book. I was afraid of sharing something so personal with "the world." Plus, I was still in the middle of it; I wasn't exactly sure how it was all going to end up.

I put the thought in the back of my mind, until today when I told Loni during our walk,

"Swati tells me that she keeps seeing me writing a book about my journey through my divorce." Loni replied, "Oh…and they (our Teams) are saying that it's going to be a bestseller!" We laughed.

We started jokingly saying that one of the chapters would be titled, "I Believe in Polygamy!" Yep, polygamy, because when I eventually got into a relationship with another man, he would have to share me…with myself! Haha! We thought it was hilarious.

2/24/16: I find it interesting that so many people are telling me how good I look lately. I can count at least eight people who have complimented me in the last couple of weeks. Some of them have said, "You look fantastic!" "You are glowing!" "You inspire me!"

I *do* feel good. I feel an inner joy that is hard to explain. Even though my relationship with Matt is not going well, I have a sense of peace within me. I think it has to do with my newfound relationship with myself. I am loving myself more. I am getting clearer about what loving myself looks like. No matter what happens in my life, I am choosing to feel good. I am taking better care of myself. I am getting clearer about what I want my life to be like, too, and I know that I am creating it at some level. I know that it will be my reality soon enough.

3/5/16: I am on day 20 of my 40-day love affair with myself. I truly feel like I am falling in love with myself. I am getting to know me more intimately. What I like. What is important to me, and who I am, both from a human perspective, as well as from a spiritual perspective. I am getting to appreciate all of me. This is so awesome! Life changing, really.

When I reflect on why it was so difficult for me to love myself, I get that it was the natural result of the constant messages we receive growing up. We are encouraged not to love ourselves from the time we are very young. We are taught from the time we are small children that others are more important than we are. For example, we are told that we have to share our toys even if we don't want to, and that we should not be selfish.

When we are little, we are also told that others are more knowledgeable than we are. For instance, we have to listen to and do what grownups say because they know more than we do. And later in life, we are told that others (i.e., parents, teachers, doctors, experts, religious leaders) know better than we do, and therefore, we have to look for answers outside of ourselves. No wonder it is so difficult for us not only to love ourselves, but also to trust our inner guidance!

Women have this primal instinct to be pleasing towards men in order to survive and be protected and provided for. We are also taught to give our power away to men and male authority figures (i.e. husbands). For hundreds of years, women have had to be financially and physically dependent on men. This is slowly changing, but...this is still very much ingrained in our psyche. I saw both my mother and grandmother endure marriages where they were unhappy because they didn't believe they could support themselves financially.

And as mothers, we are told that we need to sacrifice ourselves for our children because their needs come first, before ours. For many mothers, this belief continues manifesting throughout their lives, even as their children grow up.

I could easily see these patterns in others, like my mom and grandmother, but had not seen that I was repeating the same patterns until my Team brought it up to my attention through Swati last December.

I am so glad I am breaking free from these patterns! They are disempowering and do not reflect Who I Really Am or who I want to be. I am so grateful to my Team for helping me shift these limiting beliefs and fears I've held.

I actually see how I am like a caterpillar that went into the darkness of its cocoon in order to go through a transformation. I can feel how a new me is being shaped. I can almost sense my beautiful wings being formed. I know that at some point I will go out into the light, spread my wings, and fly.

***

As I told you in Chapter 4, I learned the truth about Matt's behavior in mid-March. Remember that upward spiral I told you about? My experience in March is a perfect example of it. One day, I felt angry and overwhelmed. But because I had started my 40-day program beforehand, it was easier for me to **refocus** myself after that, even after my sickening meeting with Matt's best friend at the ice rink.

With the help of my friends and my Team, I focused on loving myself rather than on my anger. And this helped me to reframe so many things in my life: my relationship, and everything else that didn't serve me.

***

3/13/16: I need a new car. My good old Toyota Sienna minivan is not working so well for me anymore. Some doors are not opening when I press the "open door" button. There is also something wrong with the electrical components: the GPS, the radio, and the backup camera. Sometimes they turn on all by themselves, but never when I need them to. I also feel like I've outgrown the minivan and everything it represents: mothering, young children, driving the kids everywhere, and even the license plate, "WSEMOM." My minivan and I are not a vibrational match anymore.

Oh, my Team is telling me that my car is a metaphor for my relationship with Matt. They say,

Your minivan, just like your relationship with Matt, is no longer serving you. You are not an energetic match anymore. They are breaking down and you are ready for something new!

I've gotten very clear on what I want in a new car (just like I am on what I want in a new relationship). I recently test drove a Hyundai Santa Fe and loved it. Oh yeah! I want a Santa Fe Sport, Silver, with a backup camera, heated seats, and a navigation system. I would love a sunroof too.

I *am* grateful for my minivan, just like I am grateful for my marriage. They have served me well for many years. I love, value, and honor them. They helped me get to where I am now. But at this point, I want so much more! As for a car, I want reliability in a smooth, comfortable, easy to drive, sporty, and sexy vehicle that gets me to where I want to go in an empowered, joyful, and fun way. Yep. I am ready for a new car…and a new life!

3/14/16: When I saw my friend Amy today at Alex's school, she said something to me that made my heart recognize the truth in her words. It also gave me hope for the future. She said that when I was leaving her house a couple of days ago, she heard a voice telling her, *"Dumari will look back at this time and say, 'This was the best thing that ever happened to me.'"* "I hope so," she thought to herself.

Amy's comment reminded me of what my friend Loni saw in her mind's eye this past week. We were talking to our Teams and she said, "Oh Dumari, I see you getting re-married. And you are so happy! And you have a lot of friends. There are a lot of people at your wedding."

Even though my girlfriends were giving me glimpses into a possible future, something within my heart recognized the truth within their comments. I've grown so much from this experience. Also, by letting go of my relationship with Matt, I am now free to meet a wonderful man who will be a good match for me. A man who loves me like I am learning to love myself. I really have Matt to thank because I would not be the Dumari I am becoming without going through the challenges and painful experiences I have gone through with him. My growth and future awesome relationship would not be possible without this difficult time that I am living right now.

3/15/16: I feel like I've lived five lifetimes in the last five weeks! So much has happened within me.

It's been a little over a week since I started getting glimpses of what was going on with Matt last year. It has been an emotionally intense week for me and I am grateful I reached out to my circle of positive support. I started my day talking to Loni this morning, had a massage with Jewelie, and then visited my dear friend Amy. I also got texts from Dad and Swati, and ended my day talking to my Team.

By the end of the day, my Team suggested I take a cleansing shower before going to bed to clear the heavy emotional energy and the thoughts that kept creeping in. It was really helpful to envision the water in the shower cleansing away everything that bogged me down. The water was washing the heaviness within me at all levels: energetically, mentally, emotionally, and physically. After my shower, I felt squeaky-clean. They also suggested I choose to see both Matt and myself through the eyes of God...with unconditional love, which I did. Doing this opened my heart and soothed me.

Yes, I am so supported and loved. I am super clear, too. I love how my Team takes care of me. Not only do they give me suggestions on how to take care of myself, but they also help me gain clarity. They have given me specific details about what's been going on with Matt and with myself, and it feels so empowering to know the truth. I feel free! No more secrets. No more wondering. Now I know.

3/16/16: It's already been 30 days since I started having a love affair with myself, and I loooove it! This has been one of the best things I've done for myself. What a beautiful experience I've been having.

I love taking the time to get to know me—*really* know me. It's like I am starting to date someone very special…and it just happens to be *me*. LOL! Like when you first meet someone you like. You want to hang out with them more. You have dates with them. You like having conversations to get to know them. You enjoy their company. You look forward to being with them. You start feeling a deeper connection with them, and there's a special, warm feeling inside of you when you think of them. This is what I am experiencing with myself.

You may even say, "I love you," which I am telling myself often, too. It makes me giggle! Yes, I do love myself. I like me. I like being with myself. I am pretty special. Just saying this makes me smile! It feels really good.

3/17/16: My Team suggested I refocus again on what I want moving forward. Three things came to mind: Ease, Highest Outcome (for all involved: myself, the boys, and Matt), and the Best Parenting Relationship Matt and I can have.

They invited me to get detailed once again as to what each of those three things looked and felt like. So I wrote down a detailed list under each of these.

3/21/16: I am continuing to receive divinely inspired messages coming to me from many sources. Today, a couple of them were in my inbox.

One of them was from Peggy Black and her Team reminding me that "The energy of love in its purest form is the most powerful frequency in the universe. It is the divine thread, the cosmic connection with the All That Is, Divine Source" and that "love in its truest divine form is the expression and feeling that when you meet another, you honor and recognize that they are divine," but "often (we) are unable to see one another clearly and fully for the divine beings that (we) truly are."

The other email from Neale Donald Walsch reminded me to connect with and trust my inner guidance.

> The wisdom, the insight, the answer you have been waiting for is waiting for you. It is already inside of you. In fact, you may have already "heard" it and not believed it.
>
> If you want to be clear about this answer, simply write your question, condition, or problem down on a piece of paper tonight, then pick up the paper tomorrow morning and compose a calm, wisdom-filled response.
>
> Don't be surprised if you surprise *yourself* with the answer you receive.

3/24/16: I tried again. During our previous marriage counseling sessions, Matt mentioned the things I did that bothered him, especially not following through when parenting our boys. I decided to give it another try. I once again changed my behavior to meet his expectations. The last couple of weeks, I've been making sure I follow through with everything and check with him to see if he "approves."

At the same time, I wanted to value myself by doing my best to incorporate what I feel is the right approach to parenting and communicating with the boys, which sometimes has the "follow through" look different than Matt's preference. To me, coming up with a follow through plan together with the kids is really important in order to instill a sense of trust, respect, and responsibility between them and me. I was trying to honor Matt's wishes without sacrificing my own. This was hard for me to do, and I did find myself looking for his approval.

My BIG "Aha" moment came when I realized that even after changing my behavior once again to meet Matt's needs, he did not change his to meet any of my requests for things that I needed in a relationship: open and honest communication, physical affection, partnership, lightness, and play. He did not make any attempts to meet any of *my* needs in the last few weeks.

It is now so very clear to me. I can't do this anymore. I can't keep betraying myself. I remember my Team saying to me before, *The universe is set up to fail you when you fail yourself. When you betray yourself, you'll find others betraying you. The universe will help you realize this by reflecting back to you how you are treating yourself. This is a gift. Remember that no one outside of you is the source of anything you desire. You, Source within you, are the source of everything you want.* Now, they've said it again.

Interesting how I needed to be reminded again. Thank you, guys! Once I had the clarity (again!) that the best next step for me was to get a divorce, it was easier to refocus. At least I know where I am headed now.

Thank you for the reminder in my email inbox, too! From Neale Donald Walsch, the email read:

> On this day of your life,
> Dear Friend, I believe God wants you to know...
>
> ...that yearning for a new way will not produce it.
> Only ending the old way can do that.
>
> You cannot hold onto the old all the while
> declaring that you want something new.
> The old will defy the new;
> the old will deny the new;
> the old will decry the new.

There is only one way to bring in the new.
You must *make room* for it.

3/26/16: During this journey I've been forgiving myself frequently. It's been part of loving myself. Whenever I've felt critical of myself or when I've regretted thinking, saying, or doing something, it's been important that I forgive myself for it.

Now, I am forgiving myself for all the times I:

- Allowed myself to be disrespected
- Allowed myself to feel powerless
- Allowed myself to be treated like a doormat
- Allowed myself to be taken for granted
- Did not listen to my intuition
- Did not speak up
- Did not value myself
- Did not love myself
- Did not like myself
- Did not protect myself
- Did not care for myself

- Did not respect myself
- Did not believe in myself
- Criticized myself
- Thought I was not good enough, beautiful enough, smart enough, etc.
- Thought there was something wrong with me
- Thought I wasn't worthy to be treated with love
- Was hard on myself
- Had forsaken myself
- Let myself down
- Gave in to fear and its manifestations (worry, doubt, judgment, etc.)
- Hurt others

I find that bringing in the energy of love and acceptance through this self-forgiving process helps me open my heart to heal myself at an even deeper level. So I am affirming, "Even though I (state the above thing I am forgiving myself for), I deeply and completely love, accept, and forgive myself."

I feel cleansed. I feel open. I feel light.

I can feel the power of Love healing me.

3/28/16: After dropping off John at school this morning, I went home to write in my journal. While writing, I suddenly got very sleepy. I lay down on the couch and started hearing a song. I immediately knew that it was my Team giving me a message, so I paid attention to the words. It was Peter Cetera's song, "Hard to Say I'm Sorry." I sensed that my Team wanted me to know that sometime soon Matt would feel this way.

4/3/16: I talked to my friend Jewelie today. She said something that made me realize I wasn't really valuing myself within my family. I had mentioned that a part of me felt bad for not having contributed financially to my family all these years. When Alex was born 16 years ago, it was really important to me to stay home with him. It was also important to Matt that I made our family a priority, so we agreed that I would quit my job to stay home and that he'd be the sole financial provider.

I loved being a mom. I loved being able to stay at home to be there for both of my sons in every way. I loved tending to our home to make it a peaceful and beautiful haven for my family. I loved taking care of my family and making that a priority, and still, a part of me felt guilty that I was not contributing to the family financially, especially when finances were such a source of stress for both Matt and me.

Jewelie said, “The fact that a part of you is feeling bad for not providing financially means that you are not valuing everything that you’ve done and still do for your family. You really can’t put a price on what you’ve provided because it is priceless. And if you tried to put a price on it, let’s say by hiring someone to do *everything* you’ve done for them, it would add up to be hundreds of thousands of dollars! Think about it.”

I could sense the truth in her words, so I followed her suggestion. I made a list of all the ways I’ve contributed to my family over the past 16 years. Writing down all I’ve done for my family, physically, emotionally, and spiritually made me feel really good! It helped me see what an incredible mom and wife I’ve been. She was right. It did help me value what I’ve done so much more. It helped me open my eyes to see how I’ve contributed to those I love, and as a result, it helped me value myself more.

This is not to say that a part of doesn’t still wish I could help relieve some of the financial pressure Matt and I feel, but now I don't have any regrets about my decision to stay at home to raise my boys.

4/5/16: It is now Spring. The snow has melted. The flowers are blooming. The signs of new life are everywhere around me—and within me. I've continued taking my walks, almost daily. Even if it's just for 15 minutes, I go out.

I *love* my "creation" walks. This is when I *create* my new life! Just like my Team suggested, I envision myself living my ideal life, where everything is working out for me beautifully and easily. I start my walks appreciating everything I can think of, which puts me in what Abraham-Hicks calls the "receiving mode." Then, I go through each area of my life: my relationships, my work, my body, and anything that comes to mind. I consciously appreciate it all. Sometimes, I bring my cell phone and listen to a YouTube video from Abraham-Hicks, a meditation, or an inspirational talk. I do whatever I can that makes me feel good!

***

Even though that Early Spring was incredibly challenging, I was finding it easier to refocus on what I want to create in my life, and to direct my energy towards that. I felt clearer than I had in a long time.

I had adjusted my vision, and was able to regain my focus, clarity and direction.

Throughout the process, I fell in love with myself more and more. I could feel my inner light getting brighter.

***

Divine Insights from my Team

In order to move forward towards your highest possible future and everything that you wanted, you needed to shift your focus away from the reality you were living and more towards the life you really desired.

During this phase, you redefined self-love, and you discovered what you truly want. You started putting yourself first and making decisions from a place of love rather than a place of fear. You listened to and honored your basic needs and heart's desires.

This clarity of vision—along with the energy you directed towards it with love—gave you great momentum to shift your life in that direction.

As you ***Refocused****, you allowed the energy of those new thoughts to manifest into your reality. You were tuning your radio dial to the station where your favorite song was playing. You started dancing your way towards your freedom and empowerment, all while singing your song of Self-Love and Joy.*

Chapter 6: Centered

"Your vision will only become clear when you look inside your heart.
Who looks outside, dreams; who looks inside, awakens."

—Carl Jung

In the Spring, I started to re-awaken to myself. Spring and Easter are a period of rebirth, and that's what I felt was happening to me. During this time, I was birthing the new me and was able to connect more deeply with the messages I'd received, like my Team's message that I was the source of Love in my life.

When I Refocused, I connected to myself in a very intentional way. Through my routines of self-care and self-love, I was creating a connection to my True Self—a stable place that I could come back to whenever life, emotions, or stress pushed me off balance. My spiral of progress was reaching upwards and upwards. I felt Derailed, Isolation, and like a Victim much less often.

Finally, I was **Centered.** As I started reconnecting with my soul's vision for me and my life, I started taking action from that place. I continued healing parts of myself. I made the decision to get a divorce official, even though others advised me against it. I continued getting messages that helped me heal at a deeper level and guided me towards creating my highest future.

My emotional healing became physical, too. I had lost hearing in one ear when I'd learned the truth about Matt, and eventually, a cough came with it. In order to heal the pain, I needed to check in with my Team and to listen to my body. Soon,
I was feeling stronger, so I added an extra intention to my workouts: to have my body reflect the inner strength I was feeling inside. I let go of so much fear and many limiting beliefs during this time…I felt I was getting stronger inside and out.

Moving into this phase, I still needed to be very gentle with myself. There were still many unknowns ahead of me, and there was also a lot of work to do and more clarity to gain. As I contemplated telling the kids, dealt with self-doubts about my own ability, and continued to practice speaking up, the lessons

I was learning became even more clear. Finally, I could take joyful steps towards my new life. I forgave Matt, and I started packing up the house.

***

3/15/16: I've had a cough for some time now. I talked to my soul today and shared that I am tired of this annoying cough that's draining me. It makes me feel weak. I can't breathe easily. Can't speak easily. I often choke. My ear has also been affected. It is clogged and keeps ringing; I can't hear easily.

My soul told me that this cough had to do with a part of me, a little girl, who feels sad. She is grieving. She feels abandoned. Alone. She wants so much to be loved. She does everything she can to be a "good girl." She does everything "right." But she's noticed that no matter how good she is, she is still not loved—not lovingly hugged, not appreciated. She is so sad because she thinks that no matter what she does, she'll never be good enough to be completely loved. I decided to connect with my little girl.

When I did, this is what she said.

"I just want to be loved. I want to be seen, heard, and cherished for being me. I am so sad. I don't know what else to do to be loved. Am I not good enough? I think I am! But they don't think so. I decided that I would do everything right so that I would be liked and loved. I would be a good girl. I would not cause any problems. I would not bring up any conflict or cause any stress. I would stay low-key and do everything I could for them to be happy with me. That way, they would like me and love me. But I am seeing that no matter what I do, they don't. I am so sad."

I comforted my little girl. Told her that I loved her no matter what. Then, I felt that my soul had some words of healing and some insights that would help her. This is what my soul (and my Team) said to my little girl:

Our beautiful Dumari, you are perfect, whole and complete now. There's nothing you have to do to prove you are worthy of love.

We all come into this life to learn and experience specific things. You came to learn about unconditional love. Loving yourself and others no matter what.

When others don't seem to love you, it's because they are dealing with their own stuff: their own pain, and their own limited perspectives about themselves and about life. It really has nothing to do with you.

Remember, ***you*** *are the source of Love towards yourself and others. Love yourself, value yourself, and honor yourself no matter what others think of you or how they treat you. This is true freedom. This is a beautiful and powerful lesson for you to experience. Then, love them no matter what they think, say, or do. Set them free. Set YOURSELF free.*

You are getting to experience unconditional love, exactly what your soul wanted to experience and gain a higher understanding of. Who you are is pure, divine Love. What does that look like, sound like, feel like?

BE the Love that you are. You are Love. You are loved.

3/17/16: I notice that sometimes I go into judgment of Matt and what he's done. My Team has been giving me messages with a higher perspective to help me shift this judgment.

One of these messages came through a license plate while I was driving down Rt. 101A to bring John to hockey practice in

Massachusetts. I did a double take when I noticed the license plate in front of me. It read, "2MASTRS".

I immediately felt the feeling of recognition I get when my Team is communicating with me. It's a feeling of knowing: calm, inner knowing. I was being reminded to see both Matt and myself as MASTERS. Two spiritually awakened masters who have forgotten who they are, and who both agreed to go through this experience before coming to Earth in this lifetime to give our souls an opportunity for growth and expansion, and to ultimately more fully understand, experience, and express Love.

The other message, I found in my inbox. This email from Neale Donald Walsch reminded me of the way God sees Matt...

> On this day of your life,
> Dear Friend, I believe God wants you to know...
>
> ...that you are a pure child of God, beautiful in your innocence – and That this is true no matter what you may have done.

There is no offense you could ever commit that can rob you of your magnificence, or of the wonder of who you are. Yet who among us hasn't fallen from the path, betrayed another, acted unwisely, fallen prey to temptation, given in to a craving or addiction?

All of us are human. And in God's eyes that makes us perfect. Really. Just the way we are. Like 3-year-olds, looking anxiously up at some elder, wondering with quivering lips whether we'll get a spanking for breaking the rules...

The 3-year-old is beautiful in her innocence. He is pure as snow, and there is simply something that has not been totally understood, or fully integrated into behavior yet. It's okay. We don't mean to be "bad." And in truth, we aren't, not a one of us.

We're simply, sometimes, mistaken. And God loves us anyway. Immensely. Completely. Eternally.

Just. As. We. Are.

3/22/16: Today, I had my one-on-one meeting with our marriage counselor. I told him about my recent discovery regarding Matt's behavior. I said that the most important thing to me is that Matt tells me the truth himself. Honesty and trust are two of the most important qualities for me in a relationship. He asked me if I would be willing to work on the relationship if Matt told me the truth, was sorry for what he did, and changed.

The thought of staying in my marriage made me feel sick. I want Matt to heal and I want to provide a loving, safe place for him to do that, but I *don't* want to give up myself—what I want and need—again. My whole body tensed up at the thought of going back.

The marriage counselor said that the easiest part at this time would be deciding to divorce, and that the hardest parts come later...lifestyle changes, not being with the kids all the time, the possible negative effects on the kids, etc. When he said that, I felt FEAR.

Should I give up my dream relationship and being true to myself because of these reasons? I can intuitively tell that Matt would sacrifice himself, too, for these practical reasons. He would not change for me; he would change as a strategy to keep his lifestyle, for financial reasons, and for the kids. This is *not* what I want.

My Team tells me, *Give yourself some time. You do not need to rush into anything. Just continue listening to your inner guidance.*

3/23/16: My Team is asking me to write what I've learned from my journey so far. Here's what I've learned:

1. The most important thing for me to do is to Love myself. I am still learning what that looks and feels like in my everyday life. All these are part of loving myself:
    - Believing in myself
    - Trusting my inner guidance
    - Valuing, honoring, and respecting myself and what is important to me
    - Setting and honoring my boundaries
    - Speaking up
    - Accepting and embracing all of me, including my feelings as well as the parts I may not like as much.

2. I am the Source of everything I seek, like love and security, including financial security. Actually, God within me is the Source of all this. I need to realize this before I can experience it. I am still learning how to apply this in my daily life.
    - I was looking for the things I need and want outside of myself, instead of within myself.
    - My happiness was conditional, and in order for me to be truly happy, my happiness needs to come from within and not be based on conditions.
    - Guilt and shame close my heart…as does feeling inadequate. These all lead me to seek love outside of myself. The result is that I'll be looking for love in the wrong places.

3. Most times, what others do "to me" has nothing to do with me; it has everything to do with their perspectives about life and themselves…and many times, these perspectives come from a place of fear.
    - I can't control others, but I can control the way I look at things, which will determine how I feel about things.
    - If someone does not love himself or herself, they can't really love others fully. It's not that they are

purposely withholding love; it's just that they can't give what they don't have.

4. I am loved.
    - I am incredibly loved and supported by many friends, family members, my Team, God, and my Higher Self.
    - Matt's Higher Self loves me more than words can say. He took on this role to help my soul's agenda: to experience and express divine qualities within me, heal parts of me that were afraid and limited, and learn all these higher truths I just listed. His soul is also benefiting from this experience.

These insights have changed my life. More than that...I feel they have changed who I am. I am no longer the same Dumari I was nine months ago. I am different. I feel wiser, stronger, and more empowered. I feel like I am being more of Who I Really Am! And for that, I am so grateful!

3/25/16: I came up with this funny and good feeling song and dance to get into my "vortex." It goes like this...

Going through my vortex
Totally supported
Happy and at peace,
I love me, I love me.
I am free to be me
With lots of money flowing in!

It lifts me up and raises my vibration immediately. I feel happy singing it. I even created a dance to go with it. I clap and move my body, do a few salsa moves, swing my hips and even shake my shoulders. LOL! Love it. Thank you for the inspiration, guys!

***

After I found out the truth, I felt many intense emotions. I also struggled with images of Matt in my head…Images of what he'd done when he was out late at night.

However, I asked my angels for help with my thoughts. Help in reminding me of the truth of who I really am and who he really is. I sometimes forget, but they helped me with this. They reminded me that my soul wanted to experience this in order to embody self-love and self-empowerment. That this experience was an incredible opportunity to help my heart open, to experience unconditional love, and to become a master creator with my thoughts by keeping them aligned with what I really want, with my spirit, and with God within, no matter what. They said that I would also be an inspiration and guide for others thanks to this experience.

They reminded me that Matt's soul chose to go through this experience as well. We were going through this painful experience to gain a higher understanding about Love.

I felt healed and centered in many ways. My Team helped me to take care of the little girl within me who felt unloved, betrayed, and abandoned. I got to show up for her, and show her how beautiful she really is: how cherished, loved, and taken care of. It was a beautiful and healing experience.

At this time, I went walking almost every day. It was like doing walking meditations, but even better—definitely more fun! They lifted my vibration and I got to embody joy, hope, excitement, positive appreciation, understanding, acceptance, and alignment with Source.

After I found out the truth, my body spoke to me through symptoms:

- I had a dry cough, and medications didn't help. When I tuned in, it felt like grieving. I was grieving the death of my old life, my relationship, my hopes for my marriage, and my family.

- My left ear was blocked with fluid, too. There was a constant ringing. It's like my body was protecting me from hearing the painful truth.

I needed to be patient with myself. I needed to love myself through this, and to be gentle and kind with myself.

When I asked my Team about my cough and how it's draining me, I heard,

Yes, your cough is draining you, just like your constant thoughts about Matt and your relationship, about the past and your future. It's all draining you. DETACH. LET GO. SURRENDER all control. Everything is well. TRUST. Let go of all resistance and ALLOW wellbeing to flow.

***

3/26/16: I just weighed myself. I've lost seven pounds in the last three weeks! I weigh 127 lbs. This is less than when I got married almost 17 years ago…I don't remember ever weighing so little! It feels like a heavy outer layer has been peeled off me. I actually get a visual of me unzipping the front zipper of a black, rubbery body suit and slipping it off. It's like this heaviness has been lifted of me. I feel so much lighter!

I am feeling inspired to take advantage of this quick weight loss to make my body really strong. I want my physical body to reflect the inner strength I've been developing in the last few months. Yes! That's what I'll do. I've been doing gentle yoga daily for many months now. Being gentle with myself has been exactly what I needed. Now, I feel ready to build my physical strength. I am excited—I am going to start lifting weights. I am taking out my P90X DVDs.

3/27/16: Happy Easter, Dumari. Today, I completed my "40 Day Affair with Yourself" journey. WooHoo! What a ride I've had loving myself for the last month and a half. One of the best, most transformative things I've done in the last several months, definitely. My love for myself has deepened exponentially. I now know what loving myself looks like, feels like, and sounds like. I've gotten to know myself at a much deeper level, to be there for myself, and to discover and remember my magnificence. I am committed to loving myself first and foremost as I continue embarking on this adventure that is life. I LOVE me!

3/28/16: I have been developing a new, more loving relationship with my body. I feel like my body is a beautiful vehicle for my spirit to experience life and express itself. I am grateful to my body for this and for many other things, including the messages it gives me. I want it to reflect the qualities I've been developing lately: flexibility, endurance, and strength...

4/5/16: We just had a meeting with our marriage counselor. My inner guidance told me that it was now time for me to ask Matt if what my intuition told me a few weeks ago was true. My Team said it was important for me to speak up, but that regardless of what Matt said, the final and highest outcome would still be the same: we would divorce.

My Team asked me, *Do you need him to tell you the truth in order to feel peace and to set yourself free?*

I replied, "I know the highest answer is 'No.' I do not need to depend on him for me to be free and at peace...and at the same time, I thought the highest outcome involved him being honest with me. How can I trust him if he's not honest?"

They said, *You cannot trust him to be honest with you regarding your past together, but you can trust him to be fair through the divorce.*

During our meeting with the marriage counselor, I asked Matt if my intuitions were right: if there was something he needed to be honest about. I asked him twice. Both times he looked at me in the eyes and said, "No." My Team said, *He's lying.*

I took a deep breath as I felt the pain within my heart. My heart was breaking once again. He was lying to me while looking straight into my eyes. I could feel it in my gut. I could see it in his eyes. I felt disrespected. I felt devalued...and so very sad.

When I got back home, my Team said to me,

Our beloved Dumari, we know your heart aches at the deceit and the lack of honesty. But really, he's too afraid to tell you the truth. So, his dishonest answers are a result of fear.

He's in survival mode, and fear is running the show. It's not that you can't trust him. You just can't trust FEAR. Who you need to trust is YOURSELF.

It is not that he wants to lie to you. He's truly acting out of self-preservation. He also thinks he is saving you pain.

So, the outcome is still the same. You separate and get a divorce. If he tells the truth, you get a divorce because you know what is best for you. If he lies, you get a divorce because there is no trust and it's still the best for you.

You are concerned that because he lied to you, you won't be able to trust him with the divorce proceedings. That's different. Even though he told you he needs to think about himself now, he truly wants the kids and you to be taken care of. You CAN trust him to be fair with the settlements.

And then, the next question for you is, can you be at peace even though he lied to you?

I thought about it. "Well, I really, really wanted him to tell me the truth. I wanted him to respect me in that way. I feel there's a part of me that wants him to see my wisdom and power. That part of me is saying, 'See my wisdom. See my light...and yes, hear me roar!' But ultimately, I know that is up to me to feel respected regardless of what he does. I can try to make him accountable, but I can't force him to be. And my happiness is certainly NOT going to be dependent on anything he does or doesn't do. It helps me to hear you say that he's lying because he's afraid and not because he wants to disrespect me. I get that.

"Now, I need to heal the parts of me that want to continue asking him questions, to have him confirm what I know, to have him know that I know, and to have him see my power! Anything else you suggest I do, guys?"

Find Peace. Trust the process. Focus on your vortex!

"Got it!" I said and I finished our conversation by singing my vortex song...

Going through my vortex

totally supported
happy and at peace.
I love me. I love me.
I am free to be me
with lots of money flowing in!

4/8/16: I didn't know today would be the day. The day I've been waiting for. I knew it was getting close, and it happened today.

Matt and I had an argument. I wanted to get access to his cell phone account. He would not give me access. After going back and forth for a while, we knew it. We had to do this. I could not continue like this, and neither could he. We decided to make our decision final...we would get a divorce. We did it together. It felt right.

It was emotional for both of us. He cried. I cried. We hugged...for a long time. He said he was so sorry; that he never wanted to hurt me. That he was afraid. He opened his heart and showed me a side of him I had never seen before. A side of him that was vulnerable and scared. It is so ironic...I have never felt as close to him as I did today.

4/10/16: This week I went to see my neighbor who is also going through a divorce. She is several months ahead of me in her divorce process. Our meeting was totally divinely guided. Seeing where she is now gave me hope. It felt like she was giving me glimpses into my future. She said to me,

"I've never been happier. I found a house in the village down the street. I love how bright is it! We're going to be renting it and it all happened behind the scenes. Everyone has been so helpful and friendly. Whatever I need, it seems like someone just appears to help me. And they are all so nice. I've also met this guy. We're going out on dates. We're making out! I am having so much fun. I am being touched, unlike in my marriage. I am really enjoying my life again. I am here for you, for anything you need."

Wow. This was just what I needed to hear. Thank you, guys!

4/11/16: Seven days ago, I started this really cool 21-day online program: "Release the Grip of Past Lovers." I am finding it very helpful. It's helping me to connect with my sacred body and sexuality, to embody the divine feminine power within me, and to fully release Matt's energy from my energy body. I am setting good energetic boundaries, and I am getting clear about my emotional, spiritual, and physical needs and how to honor them. I feel it is getting me ready to meet and connect with my passionate, kind, safe, open hearted guy.

This is another step towards my empowerment!

***

I had a conversation with my friend Swati that helped me to see things in a new light. I met Swati right before we were both going to take the Angel Therapy Practitioner training with Doreen Virtue over 10 years ago. Back then, she lived about an hour and a half from me in Massachusetts, but a few years after our training, she moved to California. We had an awesome conversation via text. In it, my Team replanted the seeds for me to write about my experience. This is how our text conversation went:

Dumari (D): My Team told me yesterday that I would be moving this summer and to start thinking about packing in the next couple of months because things would go fast. Matt and I had an openhearted and emotional (in a good way) talk this past Sunday. We decided to get a divorce. Ironically, during that conversation I felt the closest to him I ever have.

We are taking a few days to process our decision before we tell anyone. And we're meeting with the marriage counselor next week to figure out the best way to tell the boys. I feel so at peace. The conversation with Matt was very healing for both of us. I can breathe now. I see the light at the end of the tunnel. Actually, the tunnel has disappeared!

Swati (S): This has progressed so fast. I'm so glad you both talked so open-heartedly and am so glad all this is proceeding amicably. Did you think of where you will be living?

D: Fast? Not for me! LOL! This journey actually started at the end of last July. Then, after 7 very painful months...I finally found out last month why Matt was so cold. Then, everything started going super fast. But, every day since July, I've healed a part of me, released a limiting belief, or addressed an emotion that had a message for me. It's been a "Master Course in Unconditional Self Love...from Unhappiness to Eternal Joy." Good book title, huh?

My Team said that if I had rushed any part of this journey, I would have skipped some important keys that have helped me heal and empower myself.

And now, I am ready for my vortex: for "my guy," my successful work and business, playing with friends, my independence, my freedom to be me, and even, a better relationship with Matt! And yes, I have also been getting clear on the details of my new place.

S: Absolutely lovely book title. And you should write it, too! You should write it from a human point of view, not necessarily the spiritual reasons. I fail to see what Matt's grounds are for wanting a divorce. He gave *you* enough reasons to want a divorce. But he created all the problems himself. This could have happened years ago. But at that time he decided to progress spiritually and make it all right. Now, he has created this again. Oh well. Who am I to question the experiences a soul needs or wants?

Your new place will need to be big enough for you and your boys. Show me pictures of the places you'll be looking at. House hunting is always fun.

D: Yes, from a human perspective, this was self-created by him, although I can see how I co-created some of it, too. My Team has also shown me how this was all designed by both our souls before we got here. So, it will not make that much sense if we only see it from the human perspective. There're so many gifts within this experience. It was (and still is) painful, but Matt's soul wanted to experience this, and so did mine.

I will include you in my home search. It will be fun to share it with you!

S: Yes true. And I'm so proud of you that you can see gifts while you are in the middle of this huge storm. Somehow, you are sailing through it all without feeling sorry for yourself.

D: Thank you, but you know what? Maybe part of my soul's plan is to help others "sail through intense storms" in an easier way, with the help of their Team, a higher understanding, and an open heart. I like that thought! Maybe my future book will be part of that. Did you know I've kept a daily journal of my experience through this journey, including my Team's insights, their signs (even songs they gave me & license plates that caught my eye)? It's been amazing how they helped me "sail through my storm" more smoothly!

S: Wow!! I am speechless. You inspire me. Maybe I should do what you did for my health and weight loss. It will be a fun journey if I do it your way. You actually make your divorce journey sound like delicious fun. Now I want to go get a divorce from Swami just for the fun of it!!! LMAO! Have you met a weirder person than me??

D: No, I haven't! You are the weirdest and awesomest!!!!!!!

I love the feeling of inspiring you to have an awesome and fun journey, but not necessarily to divorce Swami!

I probably should not be telling you this...don't want to encourage any ideas...but I just lost seven pounds in one month and I wasn't trying! I was just not that hungry. Which is weird because my tendency has been to eat more when I am anxious. I have taken this as inspiration to get in really good shape and strengthen my body to reflect the inner strength I've gained through this process.

S: See??? I should totally divorce Swami. I will lose weight!! Hahaha!! Then I can go new house hunting.

D: Then, you can move to the East Coast and we'll move in together!

S: Yes!!! Seriously!! You make divorce sound like something exciting. You could even coach people to go through their divorce the H.E.A.R.T.S. Way, like your other program. It will help people so much. It will help people avoid a lot of pain if they handle it the way you are. Think about it.

D: Oh wow, Swati! What an incredible idea! I know there can be so much pain within this experience...

S: I have seen so many people go through divorce and have seen how this has torn their hearts, health, and lives to shreds.

D: Really??

S: If they are coached by you during this huge transition phase, they will actually look forward to a new life. Just like you are.

D: Oooh...a part of me is getting excited at this possibility! And you are right. I know there are many who go through much pain in relationships caused by betrayal, abandonment, divorce, etc., but I don't think there are many others out there who have gone through it in the empowering way and with the positive perspective I have, with their Team's insights, guidance, and support. Thanks for the idea...I have a feeling it was divinely inspired!

S: Yes, that's what I feel—that others have not gone through it in the way you are doing it.

I noticed also that at no point did you play the blame game.
You stated facts
And speculations.
You stated feeling hurt.
But you never made Matt a monster.
Never went into hatred.
Never went into, "I did so much for him and he is ruining my life."
Never went into retaliation mode—"He hurt me, so now I will hurt him."

All of these things ARE very normal human reactions that most people go through in a divorce. And I can't blame them for feeling all those things or behaving that way. Yet, you rose above all that and have conducted yourself at a very high soul level.

If someone gets coached by you during their process, they can learn to rise above and avoid much unpleasantness.

Have a nice long chat with your Team about this and I know you will create the nicest coaching system to help people through this process.

D: Wow! You are giving me some good insights into this! Even though I don't know when this will happen, because I am still in the middle of it, and I have no idea how I would make it happen, I feel my heart saying "Yes!" I will definitely talk to my Team about it. Thank you!!

After my conversation with Swati, I felt even more centered and clear on the next steps after my divorce.

***

4/25/16: I feel I want to be comforted by my grandma. Even though she's in the spirit world, I long for her nurturing presence. I feel there's a little girl within me who just wants be cuddled and taken care of by her loving grandmother. I want to talk to her and feel her gentle, wise presence. So, I am reaching out to her…

I said, "Hi, Grandma Anna. I love you."

Anna responded, *Hi my beautiful Dumari. Know that I am here with you. There now, it's going to be OK. It will ALL be OK, my child. Know that it is natural to feel the pain.*

This is a major transition that you are going through, and even though for the most part you are staying in a positive, empowered place, there are parts of you, parts of your subconscious, that will come up to the surface to be looked at and embraced. There are fears, there are suppressed emotions from when you were a child, and there are new emotions of guilt and responsibility for "putting your children through this."

It is important that you address, look at, hear, and embrace these parts of you. It will take some time, but it is important for you to do this.

I replied, "OK. Thank you for these insights, Anna."

She said, *You are welcome, my dear. Know that I am here for you always. I am watching over you. Helping you go through this tender time.*

So I asked, "Grandma, what suggestions do you have for me? I am concerned about some things and would love some practical help.

"First, I just found out that the condo I felt I was being guided to is too expensive. It's almost as much money as what we pay for our current house! I was shocked. I am disillusioned. What can I do?"

Oh, my dear, first embrace those feelings of disillusionment, disappointment, and fear that you may not find something you like nor experience all those wonderful things you are looking for.

Know that we are helping you from over here. We are creating synchronicities to help you find a beautiful place that you can easily afford and enjoy living in. A place that makes you feel secure and safe, connected, and surrounded by beauty. A place that is big enough for you and the boys, and comfortable.

Basically, somewhere you feel happy. Relax. Trust. You don't need to know all the details right now.

I asked one more question: "So how about my clients? Some of them are having a hard time connecting with and hearing their Teams. Do you have any suggestions for them and for me to help them?"

She replied, *Relax. It's not your responsibility to have them hear their Teams, but to give them the tools, reassurance, and tips for them to open their hearts, minds, and energy to make those connections. Tell them all the ways their Teams communicate with them. It's not all through hearing. It's all their senses. It's through art, their imagination, their environment, their gut, and so many more ways. Your meditations are very helpful, too! Invite them to try them.*

I assured her, "Thank you! This is helpful. I have to go now, but I'll talk to you again soon. Love you!"

4/27/16: This past weekend, Loni and I went to the North Conway in the White Mountains for a Soul Collage Women's Retreat. Oh my goodness, what an awesome experience. Just what I needed: a weekend away with wonderful, wise, openhearted, soul-connected women. The retreat started Saturday at 9:30 a.m.…and we spent the whole day creating soul cards from magazine cutouts. These soul cards would be used as a way for my soul to give me messages. I made so many cards! I felt a creative surge of energy that was incredible and refreshing. I felt that the cards I was creating were speaking to me. It's like my soul was either helping me heal at a deeper level or giving me insights through each card. I loved every minute of it. Well, almost…

I would say one of the highlights of the weekend was the healing experience I had with Grandma Anna.

There was a woman there named Mary who reminded me of Anna. She looked and felt like her. Several times during the retreat, I would cough for a period. I've had this cough for over two months. I've never experienced a cough for so long. Then, during dinner while telling one of the women I met that I was getting a divorce, I started coughing and couldn't stop.

At that moment, Mary, who heard me coughing, said to me, "Lungs hold grief." As soon as she said that I started crying. I couldn't help myself. The tears just flowed uncontrollably...right there in front of everyone at the dinner table. I was sobbing. A part of me felt embarrassed, but I also felt totally accepted and loved among these women.

Mary, who was sitting right across from me, took my hands. I felt a shift in the energy around me. It felt surreal. It felt as if my Grandma, who is a wonderful healer spirit, was the one holding my hands. I intuitively knew Anna was holding my hands and speaking through Mary as she said, *"It's OK to cry. Let it flow. Let it go."*

After these words were spoken, Loni, who was sitting next to me, leaned over and whispered in my ear, "That's Anna. She's the one talking to you." Yes, I could feel Grandma Anna's energy and the deeper healing happening at that moment. After a few seconds, Mary and Anna let go of my hands. We were done. I stopped crying. My body relaxed and dinner continued.

That experience was incredible. I loved feeling Anna with me. I felt her healing energy, love, and caring. Thank you, Grandma Anna! I love you!

After dinner, we went to a singing bowls ceremony, and then I went to my room. Even though I was so tired I could barely stay awake, I was having a hard time falling asleep. I was having night sweats. I felt nauseous. I kept hearing in my head, "Purge it. Purge it." So, I went to the bathroom and made myself throw up. As I did so, I repeated to myself, "I am purging any and all residues of what no longer serves me." After I felt complete, I took a shower and felt so much better! I was able to sleep well after that.

I haven't coughed since. Thank you, Anna for this miracle healing.

4/28/16: Talk about receiving signs from my Team with perfect, divine timing. Today, I got an email from Doreen Virtue titled, "Where Should I Live?" My Team did it again: just the right message at just the right time. The email had a message from the angels:

"New Home. Moving is a step in the right direction for you. If you feel guided to move to a new home, that's a sign that you're getting an 'Energy Reassignment' where you're called to a different location for your life purpose."

The email included a free meditation video to help me hear my inner guidance about the best place for me to live, and had an affirmative prayer to help me: "Thank you God for clearly guiding me to my wonderful new home that I love so much and easily afford." It was perfect.

5/15/16: I've been getting ready for this day for over a month...Today, Matt and I told our boys we are getting a divorce. This has been one of my greatest concerns for the last several months: How would they take it? How would they react? Will they get really upset? Angry? Both? I knew this would change their lives and their foundation would crumble beneath them, just like mine had.

Our boys have always been our priority. I believe Matt and I stayed together for as long as we did primarily because of them.

As usual, I prepared extensively for this. I like feeling prepared. I did a lot of research on how to tell your kids you're getting a divorce: I read books, I talked to people, and I wrote a script for Matt and myself that covered all the important things we wanted to say. We went over the script with our marriage counselor. I felt calm and ready. I could sense Matt was nervous. He called the boys to the kitchen. Once we were all there, we took turns sharing the important news that would change their lives.

I was pleasantly surprised at how well they seemed to take it. They were a little surprised, but understanding. I knew they would need more time to process the news, but it felt to me that they understood. They could already sense that their parents had not been happy.

A couple of hours later, we had dinner together. They were talkative and appeared to want to connect with us. I am so grateful for how this important moment transpired. My Team said the boys would take it well. They said it would be one of the easiest parts moving forward. It was just hard for me to believe them.

5/18/16: I have started packing up our big house. It sure feels overwhelming to have to do all this mostly by myself. What will I bring with me? What will Matt want to keep? What will the boys want to keep, throw, or give away? Oh boy...so many things to decide. So many things to do.

I want to do this in the most self-loving way. I've made a list of what needs to be done and wrote the key things on my calendar. Dividing this overwhelming job into smaller tasks within a timeframe is helping me stay focused.

I also had the idea to organize a neighborhood yard sale. Even though it will add more work for me, it will feel good to give away the things we no longer need. Plus, I will have less to pack and we could make some extra money in the process.

I will reach out to my neighbors for help.

5/20/16: My Team is reminding me that *life is meant to be fun.* This is hard to believe, especially when I'm going through such difficult moments, but they are saying once again, "the most difficult moments always bring us gifts." They say, *The key to experiencing these gifts is gratitude.* They are reminding me to feel gratitude for everything going on and also, to add a little more fun into my life.

5/22/16: I am feeling Centered, Positive, and Happy. I am so glad I am taking good care of myself. I am loving myself by being gentle, valuing myself and my needs, simplifying things, doing things that make me feel good, etc.

I've kept with my morning routine, and with my walks, Zumba classes, and workouts. I've been treating myself kindly. I've also been doing these things:

- Before I interact with Matt, I connect with my heart and ask to be guided towards the highest outcome.
- I am not depriving myself of anything I want or feel like doing. I eat what I want, when I want it (for the most part), keeping in mind that I want to love my body in the process.
- To the best of my ability and when I remember, I choose to feel good no matter what. I think about something I appreciate—as simple as my comfy bed, my boys, my friends, or the beautiful day outside—or choose a perspective that feels better. For example, I think, "No matter what it seems, I know that everything is always working out for me."

- I write myself loving and encouraging notes in my journal or on my phone. Sometimes I even schedule "I love you, Dumari" texts to send myself later in the day or later in the week!
- I focus on spending more time doing things I love: my work, uplifting and empowering others, walking, talking with a friend or my Team, dancing, reading a good book, etc.

5/29/16: Even though I've had moments in the last few months where I've forgiven, understood, and felt grateful towards Matt for everything that has happened, today I was guided to do so in a deeper way.

I took my journal out and wrote him a heartfelt letter. It was not necessary that I give it to him; this experience was for me. By doing this, I not only set him free— most importantly, I also set *me* free.

Dear Matt,

We've been through so much together. We've experienced many happy moments, as well as very painful ones...especially lately. Thanks to my Team, I've been able to see the higher reasons for why our relationship became so difficult. And I can see that it was not only painful for me, but also for you.

You did things that hurt me deeply. And I now see that you did those things because you were also hurting inside. It got really dark for both of us. And for me, it had to get dark in order for me to be able to see the light within me.

I want to say, "I forgive you." And as I say this, my soul reminds me that there is really nothing for me to forgive, because I *understand*. I understand why you did what you did. And I see how we agreed to do this at a soul level, so that each of us would have an opportunity to learn about Love and about our True Selves, each in our own way.

Matt, I love you. No longer with the romantic love that I once felt towards you. But this is a deeper love; it's soul love. I love you dearly and I appreciate you. I am grateful to you for giving me the opportunity to look within myself for the love, acceptance, and security that I was looking for in you.

I thank you for giving me the opportunity to experience this highest truth of myself. If you hadn't abandoned me, I would not have looked within myself for these things. You helped me love myself more...and through this difficult journey, I also got to empower myself. Also, thanks to you, now I know what I want in a relationship with a partner, which will help me manifest it when the time is right.

I wish you much happiness, fulfillment, and inner peace in your journey.

***

Divine Insights from my Team

Being ***Centered*** *is the natural result of aligning yourself with your soul, which is pure Love.*

When you come to Earth, you know that you are Love. You come from Love, and you go back to Love. But when you are on Earth, you forget this. Life takes you off balance. Just like a roller coaster ride, it brings you up and down, side to side, and sometimes you even find yourself upside down!

The key to bringing yourself back to your center is to connect with the Love within your heart. This will connect you with your True Self.

This is what you did during this phase. Loving yourself centered you. This helped you connect with your soul and its highest vision for your life, and from that place, you started taking action.

By loving yourself more—taking care of yourself, doing things that uplifted you, and making yourself a priority—you gave yourself permission to express, value and honor yourself in ways you had not before. From this heart-centered place, you allowed God within you to express Itself more fully through you and as you. This is the greatest gift loving yourself gives you.

Chapter 7: Empowered

"When I dare to be powerful,
to use my strength in the service of my vision,
then it becomes less and less important
whether I am afraid."

—Audre Lorde

Winter was over. As I continued to take my daily creation walks, everything seemed to be in blossom. Now refocused and centered, I too was ready to step into the next phase of my life.

It was time to take **Empowered** action. With the support of my friends and my Team, I kept up confidence that everything would unfold with divine timing. I needed to sell my home, and to find a new one. And I needed to be ready to live by myself and make an independent household: I planned to find resources and support for the divorce, and for my financial future. There would be difficulties, but I was prepared to face them.

I was also ready to step into my personal power in other ways. I was ready to speak up and advocate for myself in mediation and negotiations. And I was ready to stay committed to my dream of supporting myself financially while doing what I love.

Soon, it was September, and I was on my own—a year after things had started to go downhill. But that Fall and Winter unfolded very differently than in the previous year. I had been so lonely during the holiday season when things were bad between Matt and myself. But now, on my own, I felt loved. I felt happy.

My new understanding of love—the love within me—allowed me to create a version of myself that is **Empowered**, wise, happy, and confident. I had a new relationship to my identity, and the question "who am I?" I had been so insecure and sad at the beginning of my divorce journey. I felt Derailed, Isolated, and like a Victim; then I felt Overwhelmed. Finally, my upwards spiral took me far away from those feelings.

Now, I felt strong, playful, sensual, and capable of anything. I began to embody the Divine Feminine within me.

During this period, I knew the key was to believe in myself, and in the universe. And I got to experience the life of my dreams unfolding before me.

***

6/2/16: I am proud of myself. The universe has been giving me opportunities to speak up in an empowered way, and I've been taking them! It's funny how even though Matt has been giving me many opportunities to empower myself throughout this journey, now the universe is bringing me opportunities to do so through other people. My realtor strongly suggested I lower my home's asking price in order to sell it—but my intuition told me not to. Similarly, the owner of a tailoring shop wanted to charge me for a very low quality job.

Even though it felt uncomfortable to speak up to these people who have an authority role or a strong personality, I am now able to do so with more ease. If I disagree with them because something doesn't seem fair, or because my inner guidance is saying something different, I am now advocating for myself where before I may have remained quiet in order to avoid conflict.

6/3/16: I have some big projects ahead of me: my first yard sale, putting our house on the market, and finding a new home. I am feeling somewhat overwhelmed with everything that these projects require, but I am also feeling focused. I trust that I can do it. My intention is to listen to my inner guidance to see how I can do these things with the most ease.

Things between Matt and me are less emotionally charged. Now that we know there is an end in sight, we both are focused on moving forward in the most harmonious way we can. Our home environment feels lighter, which I am so grateful for.

6/4/16: I am super excited with my body. It is in incredible shape! WooHoo! I've continued to practice yoga daily since November. I've been doing P90X since March. I do my appreciation-creation walks almost daily and go to Zumba whenever I can. All this self-love has paid off and my body is in better shape than ever—strong, flexible, and fit!

Emotionally, I am in a really good place, too. I feel energetically detached from Matt. I've done the inner and outer "work." It looks like it's working because he's been treating me with more respect and kindness than in a very long time. I feel I can breathe more easily now.

6/5/16: I am feeling a sense of peace. I feel clear and confident that I am making the right decision moving forward with the divorce. The sessions with the marriage counselor have helped me become clear about several things. First, that I tried everything I could to make this marriage work. Probably too much! But I understand that this was my process...and it was important to me to know that I had done everything I could to make it work.

And now I know that the most important relationship in my life is between me and Me (my own spirit). And in order to honor myself, I can't be with someone who doesn't treat me well or want to be with me.

There is so much more that I want in a relationship, and part of loving myself is to not give up on my needs, but to value and honor them. I need to be seen, accepted, and valued for who I really am. I need honesty, open communication, physical affection, playfulness, emotional connection, seeing the best in each other, enjoying life together, partnership, and more.

And it's not that I need these things from a place of lack. On the contrary: now it comes from a stronger place: "This is who I am and what I value, and sharing these qualities gives me an opportunity to express my best self."

I want to excel and do my best in every area of my life, and be gentle and loving towards myself in the process. I want to be able to share my bright light with someone who cherishes that. I want to be with someone who I can be my best self with—I want us to empower and support each other to be the best we can be. Oh, and I want someone who's easy to have fun with!

6/10/16: Something I have been asking for is to empower myself in the area of finances. Now that I am going to be on my own, I need to learn how to manage my finances and become debt free. My ultimate goal is to become financially independent. I know I need help in this area.

Today, I received an email with an opportunity to sign up for a 1-year group program with a financial coach. Perfect, just the support I need! I asked my inner guidance if this would help me get closer to my goals and got a resounding "Yes." I made the investment knowing that it will pay off.

6/15/16: Going through Facebook today, I found a video that caught my eye. It listed things to remember that would help me through challenging times. I wrote the list down, but my Team made a few edits. Here's my edited list of **"11 Things to Remember When Going Through Tough Times."**

1. Everything can—and will—change
2. There's a gift within every challenge
3. You are not meant to go through it alone
4. Your Team is with you every step of the way to support, love, guide, and cheer you on
5. Sometimes, not getting what you want can be a blessing
6. Allow yourself to have fun
7. Being kind to yourself is the best medicine
8. Other people's negativity isn't worth worrying about
9. You are a magnificent, strong, wise spiritual being having a divine human experience...by choice
10. Anything is possible; believe in miracles

11. There is always, always, always something to be grateful for

6/26/16: I've been so busy this past month heading into the summer...getting ready for our yard sale, getting the house prepared to sell, and looking for a place to live.

The yard sale...what a huge project! Going through all the stuff in each room, especially the basement, sorting through what we would keep, who would keep it, what we would sell, and what we would give away...it was a lot of work, but worth it. We had our yard sale this past weekend. I am glad I did it, because we got some money out of it. Now, moving forward, I just need to pack the things that we really need.

I've also been getting our home ready to sell: painting, organizing, and making the inside and yard as beautiful as possible. Our house is now on the market, and we are ready to start showing it to prospective buyers.

I've started to look at available homes in our town. Unfortunately, there isn't that much that would work for us. I am feeling anxious: I want to be moved into our new place before school starts in September. I want the boys to be settled before school and all their activities start again. Going into high school will be challenging enough, especially for John who starts ninth grade. They'll also have to deal with the new changes of living in two homes.

My Team tells me to trust; that they are on it...that the perfect place will show up at the perfect time, and the perfect buyers for our home will also show up soon. "OK. Trust, Dumari," I am telling myself.

7/15/16: I feel so sad and disappointed. I did find a place that would work for the boys and I. Matt and I acted as quickly as we could to make an offer, but someone else got it. I got the news from my realtor while I was walking a few hours ago. I cried. I thought this was it...and it wasn't. This is the second time this has happened in the last couple of weeks. I am losing faith that I will find a nice place that will work before school begins.

My angels are telling me, *Are you losing your faith, Dumari? You're not trusting us. We have some pretty good real estate angels on this side, you know?*

7/23/16: I am *so* excited! I found my place. Both Matt and I found our new homes this past weekend. And it was perfect timing—our house just sold this week!

My place is everything I wanted...and more. It's a nice condo, just a mile from the boys' school. So convenient! It is open and airy, with lots of sunlight coming in. I love everything about it: the kitchen, the living room, and that each of the boys can have their own bedroom. And my favorite room is my office: a three-season porch with windows all around it, so my view as I work is the beautiful trees in the backyard. Plus, we can move in the weekend before school starts. Oh my God! It is absolutely perfect. Thank you, guys! You are awesome!

And this is funny...Matt found a condo with the same floor plan just seven minutes away. On my wish list, I had asked for our new places to be less than 15 minutes away, so that it would be easier for the boys to go from one place to the other. What are the odds of this? With the market as tight as it is, with less than five homes for rent in our town, and we found *two* that met all my needs and wants! My Team was right: it all worked out...and I feel so blessed.

8/20/16: While waiting in the parking lot for John to be done with his hockey practice this evening, I was talking to Swati on the phone. I was encouraging her to start singing again because she loves it. She stopped years ago. At one point, she said to me, "Dumari, I have to interrupt you. I don't know why your Team is telling me this, but they won't stop nagging me until I tell you...you need to go Salsa dancing!"

"Salsa dancing?" I said.

"Yes. I don't know why. Maybe it's because we are talking about doing things we love, but they are saying that you need to find a place to go Salsa dancing," Swati said.

"I like the idea," I said. "I remember how much I loved to dance Salsa when I lived back home in Puerto Rico. And now I dance by myself in my kitchen! I don't know where I'll find a place around here, but maybe I can Google it."

"Yes, please do. They are saying that you'll really enjoy it, and that you are good at it, too," she said.

8/22/16: I opened my own bank account today! I am moving towards financial independence. I feel empowered. It feels good.

Next steps...to separate our credit cards and any other credit related accounts, and find an accountant.

8/31/16: Tonight is our last night in this house. We are moving to our new places tomorrow. The house is all packed. We already started moving some things today, but most of it will go tomorrow.

When I was by myself today, I went through each room to say goodbye. I thanked each one for the beautiful memories we had there...and the not so beautiful ones. I allowed myself to feel the emotions that surfaced...nostalgia, sadness, appreciation, joy, peace, disappointment, disillusionment, love, gratitude...so many different thoughts and feelings came up! When I was done with the whole house, I felt an important chapter in my life was coming to an end.

I put my hands over my heart and said in my mind, "Dumari, I love you. I love all of you. Thank you. House, I love you. Thank you. I wish you both many new wonderful experiences ahead."

9/15/16: I've been in my new home for two weeks now. For the first time since college, I am on my own! Actually, I had roommates in college; so I guess this is my first time ever being on my own. I *love* it! I am so happy in my new home. I feel free. Free to be me. There's no tension. No one judging me nor criticizing me. I can do whatever I want, whenever I want to. I feel so relaxed.

If I had known I was going to love it this much, I would not have been so scared about being on my own. I wouldn't have cried so much!

One of my main concerns was who would take care of the handyman things around the house. Well, I am learning how to do things myself. Good thing there's YouTube! LOL! I am learning to use a drill, change tricky light bulbs, and put together furniture, among other things. Plus, I have a super nice and helpful landlord who is helping me with things that are beyond my comfort level.

9/25/16: I am in my office getting ready for a session with a client. I am excited about it. I love what I do for work, and I am loving where I am doing it, too…my new home office! As I am basking in the good feelings, I heard my Team say,

You are now ready. You've empowered yourself from within, and you have what you need to be a role model and guide for those who are feeling lost and are looking for more meaning and fulfillment in their lives—especially women.

Show them how you did it. How you turned the darkest time in your life into the brightest. Guide them on their own journeys of empowerment from within as they learn to love themselves and remember who they really are. Show them how to fulfill their destiny of greatness!

***

When I worked to **Refocus**, my Team asked me to get really clear on what I want, and on what that would look like and feel like.

That summer, all that work had paid off. I'd envisioned where I wanted to live, and how I wanted to feel. I had already found a place in line with my needs, and living there, working with the sun and trees in view, felt as good as I thought it would.

And there was still more ahead...

***

9/27/16: I feel FREE. My Team wishes to remind me why freedom feels so good to me through an email from Neale Donald Walsch:

> On this day of your life,
> Dear Friend, I believe God wants you to know...
>
> ...that Freedom is Who You Are.
>
> 'Freedom' is but another word for 'God.' It has been difficult to find words in human language to describe That Which God Is, but 'Freedom' is one of them. Another word to describe God is...You.
>
> You and God are One. Therefore you, too, are Free.

Free to make choices, free to select your reactions and responses to life, free to be your authentic Self.

You will not have to think but a second to know exactly why you received this message today.

10/24/16: I found a mediator. A friend forwarded me an e-newsletter from a mediator in the area. As soon as I read it, I felt it was divinely guided. When I talked to her on the phone, I got a good feeling, too. Matt and I met with her today and decided she would be the one helping us move forward with the divorce in the most harmonious way possible.

My inner guidance has been telling me that mediation will work better than lawyers for Matt and me. Not only will it save us a lot of money, but it will also give us an opportunity to come up with solutions together with the help of a neutral third party. Ultimately, this will help empower me. I will have to speak up and advocate for myself, instead of having a lawyer do it for me.

One thing I like about this mediator is that she is a parenting educator: her focus is on the children's welfare, which is a priority for me.

11/23/16: Matt and I just had our second meeting with our mediator. I think this will work well. We are going to focus on creating the Parenting Plan first, and then, we'll tackle the finances. That's the area that I am the most concerned about. I've experienced fear about confronting him in this area before, and I know I still have some more inner work to do. I can feel my apprehension just thinking about it. In the meantime, I'll work on creating a detailed budget of what the boys and I need to prepare myself for those discussions.

12/1/16: The boys are adjusting well to our new way of living. They seem calm and at ease with the new arrangements. They are living with me one week and with Matt the other week. They still come to my house after school every day, just to check in, which is important to me. They are doing well at school, too. I feel relieved.

As for me...I am so happy! I am loving my new home and my new life.

12/16/16: Before our fourth meeting with our mediator this morning, I spent some time meditating and claiming the highest outcome. I thought things would go smoothly, so it took me by surprise when I got very triggered by something Matt did.

He's seeing someone else, which is fine with me. My Team tells me that she was sent to help him feel better, which helps everybody in our family. But when I told him that I was happy for him and that at some point I wanted to meet her, he said, "What if you don't like her?"

"Why wouldn't I like her?" I asked. He smirked. And when he said, "Maybe things won't be as rosy as you envision them," I actually heard his thoughts, which is something I can do sometimes. I heard, *Because she is younger and prettier than you.* Did he actually think that? I don't know, but that's what I heard.

I was so angry. His thoughts and smirk really pushed a button within me that caused a lot of intense negative emotions to surface. I had to vent. After our meeting, I called Swati because I needed to process my pent-up emotions and let them go. I knew she could hold a positive space for me while I did that.

“I really don’t care that he’s seeing someone else,” I said. “I am actually happy for him. And I don’t care if she is prettier and younger than me. I love myself, so I’m cool with that. What bothered me was the *smirk*. I bet he didn’t even realize he did it! But it is that smirk that is really pushing my buttons.”

Swati listened to me patiently, and then relayed a message from my Team. Their message was very healing and also gave me some work to do! It gave me a key piece that will be an important part of my transformation moving forward. Once again, this difficult time offered me a gift, and I just had to notice it and open it.

My Team said,

The reason Matt smirked while thinking, "You are not going to like her because she's younger and prettier than you," is because there is a part of him that feels he needs to feel superior to you.

That's been a pattern in your relationship for many years. He can sense that you are now happy, content, and over him. He doesn't like that. He feels you're getting the better deal; therefore, he needs to feel better than you somehow. Thinking that this girl is better than you makes him feel superior.

When you said you wanted to be friends with this girl, it bothered him. He'd rather you get jealous. He really does not know you. He thinks you would be pretending if you were nice to this girl. It really bothers him that you fix things so quickly inside. He doesn't think it works that way. He thinks that it's dumb, and that you are naive and out of touch with the real world.

Dumari, you changed yourself to accommodate to Matt's ways. But he doesn't see that. For him, you are just not good enough, not sexy enough, not smart enough, not interesting enough, not glamorous enough, not fun enough. For him, it is your fault he did what he did.

It is important that you reconnect with the fun, lighthearted, sensual Puerto Rican girl within you. This is part of your journey of empowerment. You are reclaiming and redefining your identity, and this will connect you with the Divine feminine power within you.

Put makeup on. Let your hair down. Go shopping for new clothes that show off your beautiful body. Stop hiding it under baggy clothes. You've worked hard to get your body in the shape that it is: now show it off!

"Wait a moment," I stopped them. "You are telling me to put makeup on and go shopping for clothes that show my body off?!"

Yes, they said.

"But that would be vain and frivolous. Why focus on my body in that way? I know I am not my body, but a spirit in this body, so why would I want to focus on my physical body to decorate it and bring attention to it in that way? I find it hard to believe this message is coming from angels!" I said jokingly, but seriously at the same time.

You like decorating your home and showing it off, right?

"Yes, I do," I replied. "For me my home is my sacred sanctuary. I love making it look beautiful."

And your body is the house of your soul. Just like you love decorating and showing off your home, decorate and show off the home of your soul.

"Oh. When you put it that way, it makes sense to me," I said, thinking they had a good point.

You are done with the "soccer mom" look. Even your boys will be happy—surprised, but happy to see your transformation.

If you continue with the "soccer mom" look, you'll attract a "soccer dad." That's not what you want. You have created an attractive, sensual partner in your vortex, and you need to match that. He will not "see" you unless you are a vibrational match. The real Dumari is very sensual. Let that part of you come out. Salsa dancing will get you in that vibe. Dress to show your sensuality and beautiful body. It's all part of embodying the power of the Divine feminine.

Dumari, what you have done with your body, sculpting it to look so fit and strong, is very attractive. It's a different attractive than the young, glamorous, pretty girl. Yours is a strong, fit, beautiful, sensual, mature hotness that is very attractive to the type of man you want in your life. You just have to shift the way you've seen yourself all these years...and start showing more of your playful, beautiful, sexy self!

Shifting the way you see and project yourself is going to be easier than you think. You just have to be yourself. Connect to the priestess goddess within you. There's lots of sensual, sexual, powerful energy there for you to tap into.

Don't worry our dearest, your time is coming soon...and the timing of your encounter with "your guy" has been divinely orchestrated, so that it is for the highest outcome, taking everything that is going on in your life into consideration. Trust us. We are on it!

In the meantime, continue preparing yourself to meet him. Continue shifting your vibration to match the type of relationship you really desire. Continue embodying all the qualities that you wish to experience: sexiness, sensuality, independence, and freedom. Be the capable, confident, smart, loving, kind, accepting, playful, funny, lighthearted woman you are. Follow your desire to put aside Matt's opinions and actions, and to have a successful business, to make an impact on the world and your clients, to make money, to strengthen your bond with Alex and John, and to take good care of yourself. Have fun, and enjoy your own company.

12/17/16: I heard my Team's message yesterday and I am starting to do my "homework." I am going shopping today!

At first I was concerned about spending money on clothes for myself, but then I remembered I had been saving some money in a glass jar for a "rainy day." Just like my grandmother used to do. I heard my Team say, *This is the rainy day you've been saving for...and actually, there's a rainbow coming out now.*

As I was getting ready to go out shopping, I was going to put on a fleece pullover top. The zipper would not zip! I guess my Team really wanted me to start practicing dressing nicer today, so I put on a different top. Then, I debated putting makeup on. I heard them say that I had to start getting used to it *now*. So, here I was...wearing a nice shirt and makeup to go shopping.

I went to Marshall's first. But I was not having that much fun. I was still having a hard time determining if something was "soccer mom" material or not. I needed help! I asked my Team for assistance.

I then got an inspired idea to leave Marshall's and go to White House Black Market a few miles down the road. I left Marshall's and headed to the outlets. What a fantastic experience I had there! My Team really got some earth angels to help me.

When I went into the store, before I knew it, two women who worked there were putting together nice outfits and checking on me every few minutes to give me whatever I needed. They were giving me their opinions, more ideas, and more outfits to try on. They gave me the biggest dressing room and a rack. I felt like a rock star! And my new look was definitely chic, no soccer mom to be found.

I got myself new clothes and a totally different look that I love! Plus, I was able to use a gift card Matt gave me over five years ago to use at that store...a great bonus.

This was so much FUN! Thank you, guys. You outdid yourselves! And I am also proud of myself for following through with your guidance so quickly. Job well done.

12/31/16: Tonight is New Year's Eve. My boys are with Matt. A few weeks ago, I started wondering what I would like to do to welcome the New Year. This would be my first time spending New Year's Eve without Matt or the boys. Even though I wasn't sure how I would feel tonight, I knew it would be a tender time.

I had received a few invitations from family and friends to spend the evening with them, so I had several choices. I asked my inner guidance what would feel the best. I heard my Team say,

We highly suggest you spend New Year's Eve by yourself. You can have a special ceremony to embrace, release, and celebrate everything you went through in 2016: the ups and downs, the challenges and the successes, the pain and the joy, and everything in between.

Then, welcome the New Year by clearly stating what you wish to experience in every area of your life in 2017. These intentions will be very powerful at this time, and you will be adding extra energy to manifest them. Welcome your manifestations with open arms and an open heart!

“Very cool!” I thought. So here I am…staying home tonight and I am excited about it. I have already started filling out my 2017 My Shining Year workbook. Going through the first part earlier this week helped me reflect more deeply on my experiences from last year, which will help me have a beautiful 2016 Closing Ceremony.

Now I am clearer about:

- What beautiful lessons I learned in 2016
- What transformed me this year
- What I am letting go of
- What I am embracing
- What incredible things I discovered about myself
- What 2016 led me to
- What I am proud of myself for
- What I am grateful for

For my ceremony later tonight, I will create a sacred space for myself. I will light a candle and connect with my soul and my Team. Then, I’ll read my reflections on last year’s experiences with the intention to feel gratitude for everything that happened and release it with love.

After I do this, I will state my heart's desires for each and every area of my life: my relationships, my health and body, my work, my finances, my home, and my spiritual connection. I've been able to get very clear on what I want on each of these areas and I am looking forward to this powerful time helping me welcome these into my life!

1/1/17: Happy New Year, Dumari!

Last night's ceremony was awesome. It felt so good to release everything that transpired last year, with love and gratitude. And it felt amazing to claim all the wonderful things my heart desires for this coming year! I wonder what it will look like...

1/15/17: During my walk today, I had a powerful insight:

I don't have to be perfect. I just have to be myself! Who I am is lovable, beautiful, and worthy, just because I exist. There is nothing I need to do to deserve love or to have my heart's desires come true.

I AM God expressing Itself in human form. And while in human form, I am perfectly imperfect. What and who I am is Love, the most powerful force in the universe. In this lies my power. I am the power of Love!

My intention is to continue to have a deeper understanding of this truth and to experience it in my daily life.

2/14/17: Happy St. Valentine's, Dumari! Here's a love poem from me to "you."

I am choosing to love you today.
Love you for no reason at all.
Just because you are a ray
Of Divinity, of God, in this ball.

Your innocence, your joy and love
Are a pleasure to witness.
The bright light that you are
Shines out for all to experience.

Yes, you are Divine Love in action.
A gift to me, to all, to God.

Enjoy this gift of love and passion.
Play, Connect, Serve and Love,
And by all means have FUN!

Create with Joy and muse.
This is my gift to you.
'Cause I am choosing to love you,
Love you for being You.

2/23/17: Dad came to visit me last week. It has already been a year since his last visit. And even though we've stayed in touch over the phone, it was really nice to see him again. This time around, he helped me gain more clarity and confidence in several areas, most importantly getting a new car and shifting my mindset about money to help me in my mediation negotiations.

Dad helped me see that there was a part of me that believed I should only ask for the minimum to fulfill my basic needs. He reminded me that I deserved to have more than just my basic needs met. Not to take advantage of Matt—I would still be considerate of his financial situation—but to take care of myself and affirm to the universe my abundant nature.

We spent some time reminding ourselves of our true spiritual abundance and what that would look like in our physical reality. Dad also helped me go through my budget and apply a more abundant mindset towards it. Moving forward, I decided to look for ways to help myself become a vibrational match to the abundance that I desire to experience in my life.

And for fun, we visited some car dealerships to have me practice how to negotiate a good deal on a car.

3/8/17: My Team has been telling me to go Salsa dancing for the past six months, and I finally went tonight! Oh my…I wish I had listened to them sooner. I absolutely loved it! It was *so* FUN.

I Googled Salsa dancing close to me and found a place just 20 minutes away. Easy. I bet my Team knew about this place. Haha! The place offered a one-hour group lesson (for just $5!) and two hours of free dancing afterwards. I loved the environment; it was really friendly and welcoming. And there were some great dancers, too!

Feeling the music within every cell of m move to the sensual music was totally nou brought me back home. I had forgotten how g dance to Latin music in such a setting. It helped with the Puerto Rican girl within me that loves to d

Thank you, guys, for pushing me to move beyond my co zone. I felt proud of myself. Even though I had no idea whe the place was (I would have to rely on my GPS), and I didn't know anyone there, I still went by myself. I trusted my Team that I would be safe and that everything would be OK. And it was more than OK. It was AWESOME. I will go every week! Yep, I am treating myself to Salsa dancing. It will be so fun.

3/15/17: My relationship with Alex, who's now 17, is the best it's ever been. I am so happy about this. He is treating me with respect and kindness. I can sense he's valuing me in a way he didn't before.

In the past, he didn't talk to me much. Now he comes home from school and shares things that are going on in his life. Sometimes he calls me into his bedroom because he wants to show me things he is interested in or things he is doing at

. And he talks to me for a long time! He's even asking me t spiritual concepts. Something I never thought would pen, but that I hoped for. I love it!

ot that long ago, I was afraid that my sons would start treating me like their father had. I had started seeing signs of this. I needed to change that…by teaching them how to treat me. Even my Team brought it up to my attention. Plus, I didn't want my boys to repeat this pattern with their future partners.

Now John, my 15-year-old, is even coming to me to ask me about relationships and girls. I am taking advantage of this opportunity to share what I've learned while strengthening our own relationship.

I am so proud of myself for setting a different example for them. I can see how they see me differently now. They value me more. Respect me more. Appreciate me more. They even like spending time with me, something that is not common for teenage boys. This is the best gift I could have asked for! I feel so happy and grateful.

3/20/17: Matt and I are almost done with all our divorce negotiations. Coming up with the financial agreements was the most challenging part out of the whole process with the mediator, just like I had anticipated. But I am so proud of myself for advocating for myself and not giving in in the areas that were the most important to me.

There were many times when I felt the fear in the pit of my stomach, especially when I had to speak up because I disagreed with something Matt was saying or proposing. But I did my best to speak from an empowered place. I worked through my fears and resistance. Even though it was difficult, going through this process was so empowering. I also learned a lot about negotiating and coming up with a fair settlement.

I am grateful to Matt for working with me to come up with agreements that take care of the boys and me in a fair way.

3/27/17: I did it! I got a new car today. And I did it by myself. My manifesting worked…and after all the research I did in the last year, I ended up with a Silver Santa Fe Sport, which is what I said I wanted over a year ago. So funny. I am really proud of myself. Good job, Dumari! Now, enjoy your new ride…

***

Everything in my life was coming into place. My wishes for the new year were coming true: my relationship with my boys was wonderful, and I felt happy. I was still enjoying living on my own.

Of course, I'd also asked for the highest outcome in my career. Soon, something I hadn't quite expected happened. A year earlier, I had spoken to Swati, who told me she foresaw me sharing the story of my journey with other women. Her words were in the back of my mind, but I had no plans to act on them—I just wanted to continue to live my life, and to work with my clients on connecting to their Teams.

But I guess my Team had different plans: at the end of March, I opened my inbox and found an email offering me an opportunity to write a book and create an online course based on it. When I first read the email, I could feel it was divinely guided. I started thinking about what I could write about and teach, "Probably how to connect with your Team," I thought.

But when I asked my Team what they thought about my idea, they said, *No, you will write about what you've gone through.*

"What do you mean?" I asked. "Loving myself?"

Yes, and also how you got there. It is now time to write about your divorce journey.

"Now? So soon?" I asked them.

They said, *You have your diary. Everything you went through is in there. Get typing! Everything you need will come your way. You will be helping women who are going through or have gone through a divorce to regain their identities. You will empower them to fulfill their purpose and find their greatest life. You will help them to go from a place of confusion to a place of self-love and empowerment. You'll help them see how this can be the best thing that ever happened to them!*

Everything was falling into place. I told them, "OK guys. I feel excited. I'll do this, but I'll need help. I have many questions about how I am going to make this happen. I trust you, and I trust the process. I trust that everything is unfolding in the highest way possible. I surrender to the higher plan being expressed through me and as me. I say 'Yes!' to playing my part. I trust that I will be guided and supported through this."

I heard, *Yes, we've got your back.* And I saw a heavenly wink in my mind's eye.

And as you already know, this was the beginning of the book you now hold in your hands.

***

4/16/17: I woke up this morning so excited to write. I am typing all my journal entries into my computer. I feel my heart is jumping up and down with excitement and doing a little dance, too. I had no idea I would feel this way. I have a really good feeling about this book. I am getting glimpses of how it will touch many people's lives in such a beautiful and powerful way. I am feeling the love going from my heart to the readers of my book...and I feel their love coming back to me. I feel blessed. I feel honored. What a gift!

4/27/17: It is official. Today I received the signed divorce decree from the court. I am a free woman. Officially free to be *me*! I feel so grateful for this journey. I would do it all over again…all the pain, all the challenges, all the fears...for the gifts that it has brought me: the empowerment, the healing, the growth, the freedom from limiting beliefs, and the fulfillment of my soul's greatest destiny.

What a ride this has been! And I feel this is just the beginning. I am looking forward to a new life filled with joy, peace, play, fulfillment, fun, love, abundance, and many, many blessings. I look forward to the adventures ahead.

5/4/17: I am so excited: I was invited to join a Bachata dancing group that meets every Monday night. How lucky am I? I recently discovered that I like dancing Bachata as much as Salsa. I am so happy that I'll get to learn and practice this style of dance. Between Zumba, Salsa, and Bachata I am dancing several times a week now. It is so much fun!

Another thing I am grateful for is that I am making new friends…and they all love to dance. I am so grateful my Team suggested I look for a place to dance Salsa. Guys, you are awesome!

5/5/17: When I woke up this morning, I felt so incredibly happy. I thought, "Yes, I LOVE my life!" I feel so proud of myself for everything I've done to get here. I believed in myself. It wasn't always easy, but I was courageous and brave. I trusted that life was always working out for me, and that I am always lovingly and divinely supported by the universe...and my Team. I feel so blessed!

5/17/17: I innocently thought I was done with my lessons from this divorce, but I guess that is not completely true. Matt has not transferred the money for the alimony and child support yet. He's a couple of days late. Actually, I've had to remind him almost every time since we separated. I've asked him to create a reminder for himself, but it hasn't helped yet.

OK, I get it, Guys...another opportunity for me to love myself...this time by speaking up and taking care of myself.

I hear my Team saying, *Live Fearlessly.* And once again, they remind me,

When Love Appears, Fear Disappears.

Connect with the Love within your heart and let it fill you up. When you fill yourself with the power of Love, there is no room for fear. Feel the power of Love within you. Act from this place. Be fearless. Be Love.

This is helping me understand that life will continue gifting me with opportunities to "announce and declare, experience, and express, the grandest version of the greatest vision I ever held about Who I Am," as God told Neale in his book *Conversations with God*. And Who I Really Am is Divine Love.

Will I choose Love or fear? I am choosing Love! I am choosing to love myself, to believe in myself, and to advocate for myself. I choose to love others in the process, too. I remember that we really *are* one. I choose the highest outcome and affirm that everything is always working out for me. I Am the Power of Love.

I connected with my heart and the empowered Dumari within me. I sent love to Matt. I made the call. I was pleased to hear Matt say it was a misunderstanding, and he quickly made the transfer. I have a feeling this will not happen as often anymore.

I am glad I spoke up in an empowered way, with Love guiding me. Yes, I am a different Dumari. I really like this Dumari.

I am hearing my Team say,

As long as you are living a human experience, you will continue to be blessed with challenges. These challenges all bring gifts with them. They push you to grow and evolve, to develop talents, and to shift limiting perspectives. Ultimately, they give you an opportunity to choose who you want to experience yourself as.

Fear will also continue to be felt as part of your human experience. It's part of the design. But now you know that fear is just the absence of Love. Just like darkness is the absence of light. You know that as soon as you turn on the light, the darkness goes away. So it is with Love. As soon as you turn on the light of Love within you, the darkness of fear goes away.

5/22/17: My Team reminds me that my divorce journey, including all the challenges within it, was part of the plan for my awakening. It was an answer to my soul's yearning to discover and express its gifts, and to be free to be my True Self.

"The Plan of Your Awakening" (by Paul Ferrini)

Everything that happens to you
Is part of the plan for your awakening,
Including those challenging events
That force you to shift out of your inertia
And self-limiting behavior patterns.

From the depth of your soul,
You call out for growth.
You pray to be released from your burdens
And to discover and express your gifts.

From deep within your pain you call for peace.
From deep within your co-dependency,
You call for the courage
And the freedom to be yourself.

5/26/17: I received another gift today. This one came in the mail: another letter from the court. My request to use my mother's maiden name was granted. Yay! I am so excited: from today on, I am Dumari St. Angelo! Yes...I LOVE it!

A new chapter in my life has begun. I wonder what it will look like. One thing I know: it will be amazing! My heart is overflowing with gratitude for what has been, what is, and what is to come.

For this and so much more, I am so grateful!

***

Divine Insights from my Team

Empowered. *This was the end result of the beautiful journey of transformation you went through. You empowered yourself from within...with the power of Love.*

Each phase you went through was important, starting with the moment you got Derailed—when you started noticing your connection with Matt, whom you thought was your source of love and security, was weak. Then, you felt Isolated, like a Victim, Overwhelmed. You Refocused, got Centered, and finally, Empowered.

Each phase brought opportunities for you to heal a part of yourself that felt afraid, lacking, or inadequate. You shifted limiting beliefs that did not reflect the magnificent, divine spirit that you are in truth. This process also allowed you to develop knowledge, skills, and a mindset that you wouldn't have developed otherwise.

You gained confidence and resilience. You spoke up for yourself and set boundaries. You got to fall in love with yourself! You connected to and trusted your intuition, and you experienced the magic of divine help and the guidance of your Team. Your relationship with your children got better than ever, and you have been seeing the life of your dreams unfold right before your eyes.

Ultimately, you found yourself. You allowed more of your True Self to express through you and as you, and you discovered that the source of everything you need is not outside of you, but within.

Yes, your divorce journey was truly a gift...a gift of Love!

Closing Words...

"Perhaps the butterfly is proof
that you can go through a great deal of darkness,
yet still become something beautiful."

—Beau Taplin

Today, as I write the closing words to this book, I am smiling. I am sitting in my sun-filled home office, overlooking the beautiful green trees in my backyard. I see a couple of squirrels chasing each other and a few chipmunks playing around. I feel a sense of fulfillment. I am content. I am happy. I am proud of myself for everything I've accomplished, including writing this book.

I am amazed at how I was able to write this book in only two months, which seemed almost impossible when I first got the offer to write it. But my Team was right: Everything I needed was provided to me.

As I reflect on everything that transpired in order for you to be reading this book right now, I feel a sense of grace and divine synchronicity: from me going through my D.I.V.O.R.C.E. journey, to my Team suggesting that I write everything down, to receiving the opportunity to write a book, to you reading these words today.

Can you feel the divine magic within this process? My Team tells me that none of it has been a coincidence. This book is an answer to your prayers.

***

My hope is that the lessons I learned on this journey can help you emerge Empowered and loving yourself more than you ever have as you walk along your own path.

Just as the caterpillar first goes into its dark cocoon before it emerges out into the light as a beautiful butterfly, my journey of transformation led me through the darkness in order to come out the other side as a beautiful woman free to be her True Self and fly.

I learned so many lessons throughout my journey of D.I.V.O.R.C.E. Every single experience I had in each stage served me in some way and led me to my ultimate destination: empowering myself from within.

If you have gone through or are going through a divorce, are thinking about it, or are going through any other major difficulty in your life, first, I want to tell you that I am sorry. I know how painful and disorienting it can be.

I also want to remind you that every single challenge you experience in your life has a gift for you. These challenges are opportunities for you to grow in some way and to express your True Self more freely. Basically, they are opportunities for you to embody a greater expression of your magnificent spirit and to live your greatest destiny.

It is important to remember that you do not have to go through it alone. You have an amazing Team who loves you unconditionally and is happy to assist you every step of the way.

The lessons I learned and the tools I used through my journey can also help YOU:

- Navigate through your own journey more easily
- Heal from the pain and wounds you may still carry within you
- Manifest the life of your dreams!

Even though this book is about my journey of empowerment through self-love, the reason I was divinely guided to write it was for YOU. To give you hope. To offer you insights and a higher perspective about *your* own journey. And to show you that it *is* possible to go from a place of confusion and feeling lost to a place of clarity, peace, and joy!

When I first realized something was not right in my marriage, it **Derailed** me: I felt lost and confused. If you are feeling derailed in your own life, it will help to first shift your perspective about what is going on. Like my Team told me when I was about to face the Tough Mudder, "Every challenge (a.k.a. "muddy obstacle") you experience in your life brings a GIFT to you. Mud can be your friend."

I invite you to ask your inner guidance: "What is the gift this challenging experience is giving me? What can I let go of in order to receive this gift? What can I embrace in order to receive this gift?"

Soon after feeling derailed, I felt **Isolated** in my marriage. I felt alone, disconnected, and afraid. If you are feeling this way, know that you are never alone! You are always loved and supported by your Team, who is ready and happy to help you feel your true connection with Source, with Love, and your own soul.

I learned that if you are feeling isolated, you are likely looking for love outside of yourself. Instead, start reconnecting with the true source of love *within* you. Ask yourself, "How can I accept, appreciate, value, and honor myself in the most loving way I can?"

In the midst of your journey, you may be feeling like a **Victim**. This is such a common experience when we feel we have no control over what is happening. I felt helpless and powerless over the circumstances in my marriage and over my limiting beliefs, especially those that had been passed down to me through the generations. However, my Team helped me realize that I am never a victim.

You have the power to shift your beliefs, as well as your inner experience regarding what is happening in your life. When you shift your thoughts and perspective, your outer reality will start to shift, too.

Ask your inner guidance, "In what ways do I see myself as a victim in this situation? What beliefs are in the way of me being free to express my True Self in my life?"

Stress makes us feel **Overwhelmed**. And going through a divorce or any major transition can be totally overwhelming. The stressors are emotional, mental, physical, and energetic.

It's important that during times of overwhelm you are gentle with yourself. What can you do to take care of yourself during this time? What can you focus on that will help you start moving towards your desired destination and highest good?

In order for me to keep moving forward, it was important that I **Refocus** on loving myself and on my soul's highest vision for my life. These are the keys to creating the life of your dreams. Ask yourself, "How can I love myself more? What does my ideal life look like?" And most importantly, "How would I *feel* if I were living it?"

The more I connected with my True Self by listening to my inner guidance, lovingly took care of myself, and made my happiness a priority, the more **Centered** I became. This allowed me to heal not only emotionally, but also physically. Forgiving Matt and myself was also an essential component to my healing.

If you are feeling out of balance, ask yourself, "How can I take better care of myself? Am I willing to forgive myself for how I've contributed to this situation? Am I willing to forgive everybody else involved in this painful and challenging experience?"

Once I loved myself, focused on what I really wanted, and acted from a place of connection with my soul, it was easier for me to be **Empowered**. Throughout this phase I still had much work to do, and I had to trust that everything was unfolding for my highest good, but I was now starting to live the life of my dreams. And most importantly, I was happy!

I invite you to ask yourself, "Do I trust that everything is unfolding for my highest good?" If you don't, it's OK. Love the parts of you that don't, and then ask, "Am I willing to? Am I willing to trust that everything is unfolding for my highest good? Am I willing to believe that I can live the life of my dreams, be fulfilled, and truly happy?" Your answer will determine your experience. And your soul knows you *can* live the life of your dreams, be fulfilled, and be truly happy!

***

I am honored to be part of your journey of awakening to your True Self. It is truly a blessing to you, to me, and to the world.

Like I said before, "I feel so grateful for this journey. I would do it all over again…all the pain, all the challenges, all the fears…for the gifts that it has brought me: the empowerment, the healing, the growth, the freedom from limiting beliefs, and the fulfillment of my soul's greatest destiny."

Sharing the intimate details of my journey in this book wasn't always easy. Even the process of writing this book has given me an opportunity to heal fears within me: How would this book impact my boys? How could it affect Matt? Will I be judged by others who may not understand? My tendency is to be more private with my personal life, so sharing my story is definitely a stretch for me. And still, my main motivation in moving forward with it was seeing how it would help you and many others who would be inspired, healed, and empowered by reading it.

I love my life now, and I am excited about where it is leading me.

I am eternally grateful to my Spiritual Support Team. I could not have gone through my D.I.V.O.R.C.E journey in such a short amount of time and in the loving way that it happened without them.

I would really love for you to connect with *your* Team so that you can experience their love, insights, and guidance to help you in your own journey. It can make such a big difference!

In order to help you connect with your Team, I've recorded a beautiful and powerful meditation, "Meet Your Spiritual Support Team" as a gift for you. You can access it here:

www.EmpowerUfromWithin.com/book-free-gift

The journey of my divorce has given me many gifts: I finally love myself more than I ever have in my life. I healed parts of myself that felt afraid, inadequate, and lacking. I shifted limiting beliefs that dimmed my light and kept me small. I developed helpful skills and gained valuable knowledge that is helping me live my life more confidently.

I strengthened my intuition and my relationship with my Team. My relationship with my children is better than ever. I gained trust (and proof) that the universe has my back. I have reconnected with the bright light within me. And now I am fulfilling my soul's greatest joy and my life's work of empowering others from within.

Now it is YOUR turn to discover and claim the gifts within your journey. If I did it, you can do it, too. Plus, you don't have to do it on your own. Your Team is with you, supporting you and loving you. Right here. Right now.

They are telling me they have something to say to you...

***

A Special Message to YOU

from Your Spiritual Support Team

Dear beautiful soul,

We are so happy that you are here reading our words to you. We are with you now. Yes, right here with you. We've been with you for a long time. And it is our deepest desire to support you in your journey so that you can enjoy it more fully and ultimately fulfill what you came here to experience with joy in your heart.

Who you are is magnificent. You are a beautiful expression of the divine Itself. Imagine for a moment that God is like the sun: the source of pure Light, brilliant and bright. Who you are is a ray emanating from that bright Light. You are a being of light experiencing life in a divine human body—a wonderful gift.

We are here to support you in experiencing your life as the gift of Love it is. We are here to help you remember your highest truth and to experience it in your daily life.

If you are struggling, or feeling sad or confused, invite us to help you. We can support you in having more ease, joy, and clarity.

Open your mind and heart to the infinite and beautiful possibilities ahead of you.

And what would these possibilities look like? They would be YOU, feeling a deep sense of peace, joy, and love wherever you go, wherever you are.

Take a moment to imagine this and feel it in your being. See yourself going through your life feeling a deep sense of peace...joy...and love. Breathe it in. Radiate it out. Allow yourself to feel it...and BE it.

You are meant to be happy. You are meant to be, experience, and express the power of Love within you. This is your greatest destiny.

You are Love. You are loved.

We are here for you,
Your Team

About the Author

DUMARI ST. ANGELO is the founder of Empower U from Within and the creator of The H.E.A.R.T.S. Way to Divine Guidance.

Her mission is to help awaken those who are looking for more fulfillment and meaning in their lives. She reminds them of their divine identity and empowers them to fulfill their soul's greatest vision for their life so that they can wake up in the morning with clarity, excitement, and connection to the divine support available to them.

Through her work, Dumari helps individuals embrace their True Self and tap in to the wisdom, love, and practical support of their own soul, angels and guides—or as she likes to call them, their "Spiritual Support Team."

Based out of New Hampshire, Dumari offers courses, workshops, and coaching that empower you from within. She's also available to speak to groups and travel to other locations by request.

To learn more about Dumari and her work, please visit www.EmpowerUfromWithin.com.

To sign up for the **"EmpowerU" newsletter**
with ongoing messages from
Dumari and her Spiritual Support Team, go to:
www.EmpowerUfromWithin.com

***

To receive a free **"Meet Your Spiritual Support Team"**
guided meditation from Dumari, go to:
www.EmpowerUfromWithin.com/book-free-gift

54375135R00148

Made in the USA
San Bernardino, CA
15 October 2017